D1084207

THE POWER OF FIVE

FOR NETWORK MARKETING

JOHN C. MAXWELL

LIST OF RECOMMENDED JOHN C. MAXWELL TITLES

The 17 Essential Qualities of a Team Player

The 17 Indisputable Laws of Teamwork

The 21 Indispensable Qualities of a Leader

The 21 Irrefutable Laws of Leadership

25 Ways to Win with People

Attitude 101

Beyond Talent

Developing the Leader Within You 2.0

The Difference Maker

Everyone Communicates, Few Connect

Failing Forward

The Leader's Greatest Return

Leadershift

Leadership Gold

Put Your Dream to the Test

Self-Improvement 101

Success 101

The Power of 5 for Network Marketing
by John C. Maxwell

Front cover image and book design by Method & Model Designs.

Printed by BookVillages, Inc., in the United States of America.

First printing edition 2019.

Published by The John Maxwell Company
2170 Satellite Boulevard
Suite 195
Duluth GA 30097

www.johnmaxwell.com

DEDICATION

This book is dedicated to my friends in the Network Marketing industry. Few other groups have helped me consistently live out my value of adding value to leaders who multiply value to others.

ACKNOWLEDGEMENTS

Thank you to the members of the Advisory Council of the Ambassador program. You added tremendous value to this book with your input, candor, and care for its content, and I am excited to see how it impacts the Network Marketing industry.

Thank you also to my team, for helping me develop this book and bring it to life!

CONTENTS

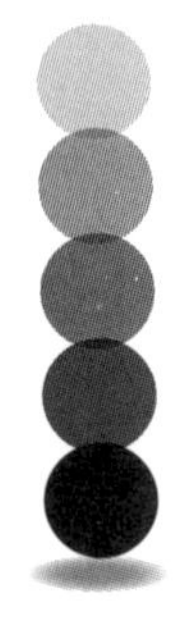

/ INTRODUCTION /

WHY YOU SHOULD CHOOSE NETWORK MARKETING

The first time I spoke to the Network Marketing industry was in San Diego. That night as I was introduced and walked on stage to speak, I immediately fell in love with the people who are a part of this industry. They greeted me with a standing ovation. They leaned into me as I spoke. They took notes of my talk and readily responded with laughter and applause throughout my teaching.

As I enjoyed my stage time with them, I kept asking myself, "Who are these people? Why are they so excited about who they are and what they do?" These people were wonderfully different from most of my audiences. They had more passion, energy, joy, and desire. They seemed like people of purpose to me.

Today, after decades of speaking to dozens of Network Marketing organizations hundreds of times, I no longer ask, "Who are these people?" I know them well, and many are now close friends of mine. I still think they are wonderfully different! Not perfect, but beautiful people who are making a positive difference for themselves, their families, and others.

I am not a network marketer. My career led me down another path. However, I have shared with others that I believe I would have thrived in this industry and would have loved doing so! My stage time in San Diego made me feel like I was "home". A place where I belonged. Today I feel the very same. It is my intention in this book to introduce you to my friends. I'm quite certain that when you meet and get to know them, you will feel like me, that they are wonderfully different.

When I was a teenager, my father taught me an exercise in decision-making. He took a piece of paper and drew a line down its middle. On the left side, he wrote the word "Pro", and on the right side the word "Con." He then told me to list all the good reasons for making a decision on the pro side and all the bad reasons for making that same decision on the con side. Then he asked me to evaluate both sides of the paper and determine if my decision would be a poor one or a beneficial one.

Like any business, Network Marketing has a pro and a con side. Many times, I have done this decision-making exercise with this industry. My discovery? For most of its people, the pros of Network Marketing far outweigh the cons!

Let me pause for just a moment and address the term, “Network Marketing”. After meeting with countless representatives from the industry through my Ambassador program, I've learned that there are keen preferences on how the industry should be summarized. Some prefer the term “Direct Marketing” because each representative goes directly to the marketplace with their products. Others prefer the term “Social Marketing” because of the emphasis on the individual as both the product specialist and the consumer.

For those reasons, my friends have advised me to use the term “Network Marketing” because it highlights both aspects—taking a product to the market through the strength of an individual. I love that idea, so I’ve adopted it for use throughout this book.

Before I give you some of my observations on Network Marketing, allow me to position myself with you. This book is the product of my close relationship with the members of my Ambassador program. These are Network Marketing professionals; men and women who started in your shoes and grew themselves and their business to amazing heights.

These are the best of the best in your industry, and they have a passion for not just developing people but developing leaders with strong values who can make the entire industry better for everyone involved.

I’ve met with these Ambassadors for a long time now, and even assembled an Advisory Council with 20 of the highest earners, influencers, and leaders from within the Ambassador program, to shape the material in this book. Their insights into what works, what’s missing, and what needs to be encouraged have turned my passion for the industry into a roaring flame. I am giving you my very best, because they’ve asked me to add value to people like you.

Since 1979, I have written books to add value to people. Over these years, I have become a "father" to many. A father desires that his children will stand on his shoulders and rise above him. I have a father's heart. I long for those I influence to go far beyond me. Lifting others up is my calling.

For many, I have become a "guide." I am a person who knows the way, goes the way, and shows the way. My favorite leadership words are "Follow me." Together we will learn and grow. Finally, I am your friend. When I walk out on stage to speak, I sit down, look at the audience, and say "My name is John, and I am your friend." How can I say that when I don't know most of the people in the audience? Because, even before I know you, I want the best for you. I believe you want the best for yourself. And it is my goal to help you get that best for your life!

So, with the help of my Ambassadors, and as both a “father” and a “guide”,

I'd like to share with you some of my observations about Network Marketing.

NETWORK MARKETING WILL...

1. ENHANCE YOUR INCOME.

The best way to control your destiny is to control your dollars because money gives you options. Or, to put it into mathematical terms, lack of money = lack of options. But when your outgo exceeds your income, your upkeep causes your downfall!

I once had a friend say to me, "I'm just one step from being rich. Now all I need is money."

Perhaps you are just one step away from enhancing your income. That step could be Network Marketing. According to the Direct Selling Association, there were 18.6 million individuals in the industry in 2017, responsible for $34.9 billion dollars in sales . The World Federation of Direct Selling Associations reported that there were 116 million people in the industry globally, with an estimated sales volume of $189.6 billion!

In short, there's a lot of potential for you.

You are positioned to join those millions of individuals, each one poised to leverage their company and its systems and products to earn income. Network Marketing offers them a chance to increase their economic potential, whether they are seeking to supplement their regular earnings, or create another stream of revenue in their lives.

My brother Larry taught me the value of having streams of income. He is a very successful businessman, and many years ago, he sat me down to talk about my financial future. He shared that ever person needs at least three streams of income, and one of those streams should be passive, or what some people call residual, income. That's income that doesn't require your continual direct involvement to earn money. After Larry's lesson, over the next few years I intentionally developed three streams of income for my life. Today I have seven streams, of which four are passive.

Network Marketing gives you a stream of income that can grow from small to large. The only limit is the amount of effort you're willing to put into your business! That's why, as I have travelled internationally, I've discovered that

Network Marketing holds great appeal in developing nations—it gives everyone an opportunity to earn money. Recently, a friend shared with me that Network Marketing has created more millionaires than any other industry in the world. I would definitely call that "enhancing income!"

2. PROVIDE YOU OPTIONS FOR YOUR LIFE.

Allow me to introduce you to one of my favorite words: options. I suffer from "life claustrophobia"—I don't like feeling confined by restrictions that life or people try to place around me. Often, we don't recognize the restrictive situations we place ourselves in until we move ourselves into unrestrictive environments.

My theme song is, "Don't Fence Me In." Freedom of choice is important to me. The word "freedom" is actually much bigger than power. Power is about what you can control. Freedom is about what you can unleash. I am not power hungry, I'm potential hungry.

Network Marketing organizations lift the lid off your potential. They let you determine how high you can go by removing imposed fences and letting you decide how far you want to travel. Many people I've met in this industry were tired of working every day to build someone else's dream, so they went to work on their own because Network Marketing values free enterprise and gives people the freedom to enterprise.

Success takes good ideas and puts them into action. An enterprising individual, willing to try something new and energetic to make something happen, will go far in Network Marketing. If your DNA is imagination and initiative, and you're not afraid to try out new, innovative ways of doing and achieving something, this industry will give you the freedom and options to do that!

3. START YOU ON A LEVEL PLAYING FIELD.

Life is filled with unleveled playing fields. Not everyone has the same opportunity to succeed.

For example, I would love to play basketball in the NBA. However, it is never going to happen. I'm too old, too slow, too short, too fat, too uncoordinated and too late for that dream to become reality. I'm at the back of the line! I'd also like to be the conductor of an orchestra, but that's likewise never going to happen. I lack musical skills, experience, knowledge and giftedness. I am at the back of the line.

The playing field in many areas of life are not level for me, or for you. As a result, there are three types of people we all encounter:

• *Those who are never going to get ready.* Time won't help them get started. They don't want to start.

• *Those who are getting ready to get ready.* They need more time to get ready. They have chosen a profession that requires more education and preparation.

• *Those who are ready.* They want to start now.

We have to choose which of those three types we want to be.

Ray Kroc, the founder of McDonald's, often said that the first key to success is being in the right place at the right time. If you want to get started today on your dream journey, Network Marketing is the right place. It says to you, "You don't have to be great to start, but you do have to start to be great."

The playing field for you is level. You are not at the back of the line because you don't have an education or experience. Move up to the front of the line. Your company's compensation plan doesn't care about who you've been—it will reward who you become. You will find your greatest rewards come when you intentionally improve.

If you have a desire to better yourself and the people you love, then you have a clear field for success in front of you right now! This industry gives you a low risk, low overhead opportunity with a high potential for return.

4. LET YOU LEARN WHILE YOU EARN.

I have three college and post graduate degrees. It took a lot of money and time to get these. While pursuing most of my education, I had to wait for the degree to have a chance to earn some money. This is not the case with Network Marketing. They allow you to earn while you learn!

The best way to intentionally grow is through practice. The best way to learn how to connect with people is to practice it. The best way to learn how to think successfully is to practice it. The best way to learn how to lead is to practice it. The best way to learn how to make a difference is to practice it.

Guess who lets you practice it? Network Marketing!

And guess what you earn when you practice? Money!

Learning and earning cannot be separated in this business. How much you earn is determined by how much you learn. If you want to earn more, you must learn more. Learning means moving from knowing what to do, to doing what we know. Doing what we know translates into making money.

5. INCREASE YOUR INFLUENCE.

Leadership is influence. Nothing more. Nothing less. To increase your influence with others you need to add value to them. When you add value to them, you begin to make a positive difference in their lives. Network Marketing gives you many ways to add value to others and increase your influence with them.

Today, with all the social media avenues, many people are wanting to impress others. You are born for a higher purpose than that. You have the opportunity to influence others. Let me share with you the difference.

Impressing you is all about me. I seek to change how you think about me by focusing on me. Influence is all about you. I seek to change how you think about yourself by focusing on you. People who seek to impress, want fans. People who seek to influence, want friends. Impressing others makes a difference only for you.

Influencing others makes a difference for them. The question is not, "Can you make a difference?" The question is, "What kind of a difference will you make?" Network Marketing will help you make a positive difference in more people than you can ever imagine. That is a worthy life pursuit for all of us.

6. MAKE YOU A BETTER PERSON.

Why do I say that? Because Network Marketing is an environment that embraces good values. When good values are learned and lived, the value of the person increases, and their value to others begins to rise. In other words, good values make people better!

The members of my Ambassador program encouraged me to compile a list of benefits people accrue when they value the right things. Because they know the industry better than anyone, I asked them for their input. We came up with a long list of benefits!

When people value...

Attitude - They will think and feel positively about themselves and their future.

Hard Work - They will experience fulfillment and build confidence knowing they did their best.

Influence - They will know they are their "brother & sister's keeper" and add value to them.

Productivity - They will sense accomplishment and be respected for getting things done.

Inspiration - They will encourage others to find and follow their dreams.

Ambition - They will be driven by a sense of purpose and feel good about themselves and others.

Responsibility - They will own their mistakes and be appreciated and trusted.

People - They will develop others and help them reach their potential.

Dependability - They will trust and respect one another and work better together.

Generosity - They will focus on the needs of others and experience joy in helping them.

Sowing - They will reap a return on their investment in others.

Perspectives - They will see the other person's point of view and be receptive to change.

Integrity - They will do things for the right reasons and set the standard for good character.

Direction - They will make solid decisions based upon their purpose and path.

Self-discipline - They will control their words and actions assisting healthy relationships.

Understanding - They will connect with others and truly appreciate and value them.

Humility - They will be comfortable with humanness and be transparent and honest.

Listening - They will create a positive environment with the same intensity they want to be heard and follow up with questions for clarification.

Connection - They will develop meaningful and genuine life-long relationships.

Patience - They will value process while encouraging understanding, cooperation and trust.

Boundaries - They will know what is expected of them and for them and feel secure.

Saving - They will remove the pressure of debt and have financial options.

Ownership - They will work hard to build and preserve their financial future.

Correction - They will be open to feedback and understand self-discipline as the essential for change.

BIntentionality - They will prioritize their actions to ensure greater success.

Goals - They will build their self-esteem by pursuing and achieving their dreams.

Growth - They will become more valuable to others as they develop themselves.

These are the values of the Network Marketing industry. It's their culture. It's who they are. Immerse yourself into this culture and you will become a better person, but you will also live a better life. I guarantee it!

7. ADD VALUE TO THOSE AROUND YOU.

Let's revisit our life changing statement: *When good values are learned and lived, the value of the person increases, and their value to others begins to rise.* When you become a better person, it helps the people around you to become better. Better people make people better!

In my book, *Put Your Dream to the Test*, I encourage the reader to ask themselves the Significance Question, “Does my dream benefit others?” There's an old Middle Eastern blessing that says, "When you were born, you cried, and the world rejoiced. May you live your life so that when you die, the world will cry, and you will rejoice." Whether or not that blessing becomes true in our lives depends in large part on how we answer the Significance Question.

The ability to answer yes to the Significance Question – "Does my dream benefit others?" - has come in stages for me. That might be the same for you. Consider how it has unfolded in my life, represented by these three statements:

I WANT TO DO SOMETHING SIGNIFICANT FOR MYSELF

When you read that statement, I bet you think it is pretty selfish, right? Your first reaction may be to distance yourself from it. I hope you don't do that, and here's why: this sentiment is not completely self-serving.

For example, the last time you were on a plane, you probably heard the flight attendants give instructions about what to do in an emergency. If the plane loses cabin pressure and passengers need to use oxygen masks, what are they supposed to do first? Put on their own mask, and then help others. Why is that? Because it is impossible to help others if you haven't taken care of yourself.

I believe the accomplishment of a significant dream comes only when a person has something to offer. This means having a place where you can learn, work and serve. Networking Marketing provides that place for you.

I WANT TO DO SOMETHING SIGNIFICANT FOR OTHERS

Which Are You?
There are two kinds of people on earth today;
Just two kinds of people, no more I say.
Not the good and the bad for it's well understood.
That the good are half bad and the bad are half good.
No; the two kinds of people on earth I mean,
Are the people who lift and the people who lean.
~Ella Wheeler Wilcox

Wilcox's poem is a beautiful reminder that we are either a plus or a minus in the lives of others. The difference? People that "lean" are selfish and are always asking, "Who is going to add value to me?" People who "lift" are asking "Who can

I add value to?" Network Marketing will help you become intentional in adding value to others.

I WANT TO DO SOMETHING SIGNIFICANT WITH OTHERS

Retired television news anchor Tom Brokaw observed, "It's easy to make a buck. It's a lot tougher to make a difference." One reason is that making a real difference requires collaboration. In my book *17 Qualities of a Team Player* I write, "Working together precedes winning together."

When you work together with your teammates, you can do remarkable things. If you work alone, you leave a lot of victories on the table. Collaboration has a multiplying effect on everything you do because it releases and harnesses not only your skills but also those of everyone on the team.

Network Marketing encourages you to dive into the "Dream Pool." There you will find others who have a similar dream to your own. That encouraging environment will enhance your dream journey.

8. DEVELOP LIFELONG RELATIONSHIPS.

The thesis of my book Winning with People states that people can usually trace their successes and failures to the relationships in their lives. Almost everything you do depends on relationships. We tend to revere rugged individuals, but there are no real-life Lone Rangers who achieve great things on their own. All the significant accomplishments in the history of humankind have been achieved by teams of people.

That truth can also be carried over to a personal level. Most of life's great moments—the ones that resonate in our hearts and minds—involve other people. We rarely experience memorable times alone, and even when we do, our first inclination is to share them with others.

Think back to the most important experiences of your life: the highest highs, the greatest victories, the most difficult struggles, and the overcoming of daunting obstacles. How many happened to you alone and without others? I bet there were very few. When you understand that being connected to others is one of life's greatest joys, you realize that life's best comes when you initiate and invest in solid relationships.

Network Marketing creates an environment for life-long relationships. There is a commonality in the people who are attracted to this industry. Birds of a feather do flock together. This chapter describes you and the people you will work with. You are discovering that...

- You are a person of value.
- You will enjoy the journey more when doing it with others.
- You do better in an environment of "people encouragement."
- You are about to meet people who will become life-long friends.

Soon after you become a part of this group you will feel like you found your "family." How refreshing to be with people who have dreams of a better life, values that are solid to build that dream on, and who come alongside of you to help make that dream come true! It's easy to develop life-long relationships with people who are traveling the same road as you.

9. EXPOSE YOU TO INCREDIBLE EXPERIENCES.

Experiences are great teachers in our life if we are exposed to them and evaluate them. As a father and grandfather, my greatest joy is giving my children and grandchildren great experiences. At the end of each experience I ask them, "What did you love and what did you learn?" The discussions that follow have become highlights for our family. Each member of our family would say that exposure to great experience has had a positive effect on their lives.

Because I am an "experience junkie," I have discovered that there are 4 different types of experiences:

(1) Entertainment - absorbed through the senses

People do entertainment because they want to sense something. This could be viewing a performance, listening to music, reading etc.

(2) Education - involves the mind and sometimes the body.

People do education because they want to learn something. This could be a classroom, conference, athletic field, etc.

(3) Escapist - completely involves the participant.
People do escapist because they want to actively do something. This could be going to a theme park, scuba diving, social media, etc.

(4) Aesthetic - involves immersion into the event or environment that is fulfilling.
People do esthetic because they just want to "be there." This could be visiting an art gallery, walking on the beach, viewing scenes from the top of a mountain, etc.

Network Marketing provides all four experiences for its people! Sometimes all four experiences happen at one of their events. Doing the business not only allows you to learn from your own experiences, it allows you to learn from the experiences of others on your team. When I talk with those in this industry, I am always impressed by how these different experiences have enriched their lives.

10. ALLOWS YOU TO BE PART OF A GREAT TEAM.

Teamwork makes the dream work! Whenever a person sits down with me and shares their dream, I get excited for them. The dream to better yourself and your life is where it all starts. When they are finished sharing their dream, I ask, "Who is on your team?" Experience has taught me two things:

- One is too small a number to achieve greatness.
- Your team will determine if you accomplish your dream.

Let me define a nightmare for you. A nightmare is when you have a big dream and a bad team! If your dream is a "10" but your team is a "4," your dream will never rise higher than a level "4." In my book, The *17 Indisputable Laws of Teamwork,* I write about the Law of Mount Everest, which says: "As the Challenge Escalates, the need for Teamwork Elevates."

You don't climb Mount Everest by yourself. It's too big! The only way to get to the top is with a great team. That truth also applies to your business. Mother Teresa said, "You can do what I cannot do. I can do what you cannot do. Together we can do great things."

Another benefit of having a great team is that when you win together, you also celebrate together. There are few industries that recognize and celebrate their people like Network Marketing! In my experience, everyone likes to be seen—people want to know that the work they are putting in matters to others. It's part of the desire to make a difference and make a mark. Network Marketing organizations understand that motivation and reward it, not only through compensation, but through awards and recognition that encourage you to keep growing on your journey.

My friend, as you finish this chapter, I hope you understand the opportunity before you. No matter where you're at in life right now, you have the potential to get to where you want to be through this industry. You will be surrounded by leaders who will challenge and encourage you. You will be surrounded by peers who will sharpen and help you grow. You will be surrounded by possibilities that can expand your horizons.

The opportunity is significant, and significance matters, which is why you should choose Network Marketing.

EXERCISE: REVIEW & REFLECT ON THE 10 BENEFITS OF NETWORK MARKETING FOR ME

Take a moment to review and think about the ten benefits identified in this chapter. To help you keep track, make a check next to the benefits that appeal to you:

Network Marketing Will...

_____ Make Me a Better Person
_____Add Value to Those Around Me
_____Enhance My Income
_____Develop Life-long Relationships for Me
_____Provide Me Options for My Future
_____Start Me on a Level Playing Field
_____Expose Me to Incredible Experiences
_____Allow Me to be Part of a Great Team
_____Let Me Learn While I Earn
_____Increase My Influence

Now that you have checked the positives, take a moment to tally the number of benefits that interest you. I'm a firm believer that the more reasons you have to chase a dream, the more motivation you'll have to see it all the way through. Add up your number, and if it's greater than 5, you've got all the motivation you'll need to start.

So, let's get started! The next five chapters will teach you the five things that will help you succeed in Network Marketing. The good news is that anyone can learn and do these five things. Read about them, practice them daily, learn from your experiences, and be ready to succeed.

You're ready to start living the Power of 5!

POWER #1
GROWTH

I can still remember a pivotal conversation around breakfast as if it were yesterday. This breakfast happened early in my career, but its impact remains to this day! I was sitting down with my mentor and sharing with him my dream to succeed. He listened patiently, nodding his head occasionally with a look on his face that was very affirming.

After I finished talking, he leaned into me and asked the question that changed my life. "John, what is your plan for personal growth?"

I pondered his question as I sat in silence. I didn't have a plan. I didn't know I needed to have a plan. I didn't even know what a plan for growth was.

My mentor broke the silence with these words:

"Personal growth is not automatic. It doesn't just happen. To grow you must be intentional."

All these years later, and those words still ring in my ears because they have proven true time and time again. *My success in life is a result of my personal growth*. As I have grown on the inside, my success has grown on the outside.

In fact, my goal is always to be bigger on the inside then I am on the outside. If that happens, my outside world has great potential. This is not only true for me but it's also true for you. Grow yourself, grow your business. If you get bigger on the outside than on the inside, your business will get smaller. If you are bigger on the inside than on the outside, your business will become larger.

You cannot do what you do not know, and you cannot give what you do not have. So how do you avoid this? Get bigger on the inside by personally growing.

Personal growth is a silent investment—it doesn't speak up, it shows up. Each and every day that you actively learn and grow is an investment in your future business, future organization, and future self as a leader. No one is going to recognize you for doing this. There are no ranks or bonuses associated with personal development. However, it will show up in who you become and what you do.

There is good news for you. Your Network Marketing organization has a passion to help you develop yourself. You will be immersed in a growth environment that will help you make essential changes to reach your potential.

But how do you know you are in the right place?

You make sure that you're in a growth environment. If you want to grow, your surroundings must be conducive to growth. If you want to know what a growth environment looks like, a growth environment is a place where...

1. OTHERS ARE AHEAD OF YOU.

We all do better when we have better people around us. I know I do. Having a model to follow stretches me. I'll bet that is also true of you. I like to say, "If you are at the head of the class, then you are in the wrong class." Why is that true? Because there is a tendency to relax when you are number one. It's why champions seldom repeat.

I purposely place myself into situations where others are bigger, better, faster, and more successful than me. As a new member of your organization, many of the people who joined ahead of you will fit that description.

For example, every month I schedule a "Learning Lunch" with someone that is ahead of me. They eat and I ask questions. My "food" is the conversation that fills me with knowledge, thoughts, ideas, and answers that I need for my life. At each lunch I ask these seven questions.

- "What is the greatest lesson you have ever learned?"
- "What are you learning right now?"
- "How has failure shaped your life?"
- "What have you read that I should read?"
- "What have you done that I should do?"
- "Who do you know that I should know?"
- "How can I add value to you?"

Forty plus years of Learning Lunches with people that are more successful than me has been invaluable. Bigger people make me become bigger. Better people help me get better. I never want to be at the head of the class.

2. YOU ARE CONTINUALLY CHALLENGED.

I have concluded that there are no great people in this world. Just great challenges which ordinary men and women rise to meet. It is meeting those challenges that makes people extraordinary.

Mountains can be moved one stone at a time. St. Francis of Assisi said, "Start by doing what is necessary, then do what's possible, and suddenly you are doing the impossible!"

We grow to the size of our challenges. Most days when I wake up, I don't yawn—I gulp! There is something before me that will require the best from me. You will feel the same once you've started your own business. You'll wonder where to start, how to make the right decisions, and likely question if you have what it takes. Your willingness to consistently lean into these challenges to learn and grow will determine your business' success.

Everything worthwhile is uphill. No one has ever coasted to success. No one has ever had accidental achievements. You must climb to the top of the mountain. You climb to have great relationships. You climb to build a business. You climb to grow.

Expect challenges. If it's easy, you should get queasy, because what comes easy won't last long and what lasts long won't come easy.

3. YOUR FOCUS IS FORWARD.

When you are moving forward there are a lot of distractors and distractions. You will notice when you look back you will see your complacent friends who want you to stay the same. To your left are shiny objects that look good but offer little substance. To your right are people who leave, thinking the grass is greener on the other side. Keep your head straight and continue walking.

Be like Nehemiah who said to his distractors, "I am building a wall. I cannot come down." You are not leaving something; you are going to something –a business that will add value to you and those around you.

I've never known a person who kept looking back at yesterday to build a better tomorrow. Yesterday ended last night! Let it go. Recently I was asked how to get rid of the negatives of the past. My reply: "Keep your mind off the things you don't want by keeping your mind on the things you do want."

Activity is not necessarily accomplishment. Focus on results, not on tasks, because you're no longer getting paid to simply do things. You're being paid to produce results. This focus on production will require you to guard your calendar closely and then fill it with what matters.

My life is filled with people who want to fill my calendar. So is yours. The question is not, *Will my calendar be full?* but *Who will fill my calendar?* Keeping control of your schedule is essential. Say no to the good so you can say yes to the best.

Recently I gave this fictitious, fun letter to my assistant, to remind both of us to focus forward and not get distracted.

> "John Maxwell thanks you for your letter but regrets that he is unable to accept your kind invitation to send an autograph/help you with your project/provide a photograph/read a manuscript/cure your disease/deliver a lecture/be interviewed/attend a conference/talk on the radio/act as chairman/appear on TV/become an editor/speak after dinner/write a book/give a testimonial/accept an honorary degree."

Stay focused. You began this journey to improve your life and the lives around you period. Do not let anything deter your focus or energy from what you have set out to accomplish.

4. THE ATMOSPHERE IS AFFIRMING.

Let me ask you a question: "Who brings the best out of you? "

Now let me ask you one more: "How do they do it?"

Usually, the answer to that second question is "Encouragement." Encouragement is the oxygen of the soul. One of the reasons I'm a fan of Network Marketing is its environment of encouragement. There are so many Network Marketing companies that have encouragement in their DNA. This industry believes in the best *for* you and brings out the best in you.

When I graduated from college my dad gave me the best advice I have ever received. He said, "John, if you want a successful life do three things: value people, believe in people, and unconditionally love people."

Wow! For 50 years I have followed his advice. I do those three things whenever I talk with people, write books, speak to audiences or lead small group meetings. Every day I value, believe in, and unconditionally love people. That's why I am a father figure to so many.

I asked my dad once how he knew when to encourage people. He answered, "If they are breathing - encourage them."

Then he added, with a twinkle in his eye, "If they're not breathing, you can stop."

One of the most remarkable things about Network Marketing is that the people within the organization want you to be successful. Why? Because when you win, everyone in the company wins. Your success is everyone's success.

5. YOU ARE OUT OF YOUR COMFORT ZONE.

I had a mentor named Bill that always asked me, "John, when's the last time you did something for the first time?"

Bill was always "shaking my tree"—he never wanted me to get settled or satisfied! He wanted me to get comfortable outside of my comfort zone.

The problem with my comfort zone is that I am comfortable in it! There's no changing, stretching, learning, or improvement. There's just...comfortable.

I constantly remind myself that there is no growth in my comfort zone and no comfort in my growth zone. This is especially true as you begin your new network marketing business—a business model where everything is new leaves very little room for a comfort zone.

Think for a moment about a rubber band. It only becomes valuable when stretched. Stretching makes you more valuable also. There are two areas that you want to stretch as a Network Marketer:

> ***(1) Stretch in the areas of your abilities and giftedness.*** I call these areas your strengths. If you don't know what your strengths are, ask those who know you well or the person who introduced the business to you. When you stretch in the area of your strengths you will be challenged. When you stretch in the areas of your weakness, you will be intimidated. If I you asked me to speak in front of 10,000 people, no problem; it's my strength. If I you asked me to dance in front of 10,000 people, there's a big problem! It's my weakness. Learn the business and attach your strengths to it.
>
> ***(2) Stretch in the areas of important choices.*** How do you know which choices are the important ones? They are the things you can change that will make a positive difference in your life, like your attitude, priorities, friends and self-discipline. James Allen said, "People are anxious to improve their circumstances, but are unwilling to improve themselves; they therefore

remain bound." Prioritize your choices to building yourself and your business.

6. YOU WAKE UP EXCITED.

Marcus Buckingham says, "People only want two things: (1) Make them feel a part of something bigger than themselves. (2) Make them feel special." Give them recognition. If those are two things you want for your life, then Network Marketing is the place for you! The people of this industry are excited about what they are doing and who they are doing it with. This creates an environment of momentum. Momentum is like the tide. When the tide is up, all boats rise. When the tide is down, all boats drop.

UNDERSTANDING MOMENTUM

Momentum magnifies success.
Momentum shrinks problems and obstacles.
Momentum energizes.
Momentum enhances performance.
Momentum makes change easier.
Momentum whispers, "You matter."
Momentum feels things are getting better.
Momentum believes wins are *probable.*
Momentum is hope, courage, energy and focus combines.

Every Network Marketing organization has four types of people who impact momentum in different ways. To be successful, you need to not only identify these types of people—you need to decide which type you want to be. Every organization as people who are:

(1) Momentum Breakers: They are negative. They say and do things that stop momentum.
(2) Momentum Takers: They are greedy. They live off the enthusiasm of others, but create none of their own.

(3) Momentum Fakers: They are the pretenders. They talk much but they don't do much.
(4) Momentum Makers: They are growing, as individuals and in their business. They love what they do and who they do it with. They wake up excited.

You get to decide which type of person you'll be. Determine now to be a "Momentum Maker!"

7. FAILURE IS YOUR FRIEND.

Failure is not a problem. Everybody fails. It's a fact of life. What *is* a problem, however, is a negative response to failure; your perspective on failure determines whether failure becomes your friend or your enemy. How you view failure determines what you do with failure in your Network Marketing business.

Cartoon character Homer Simpson summoned up the common perspective on failure when he said, "Kids, you tried your best and you failed miserably. The lesson is, never try."

It may be a funny line, but it's an unfortunate perspective many new Network Marketers embrace. Afraid of failure, they ask their friends, spouse, or family members to look at a new opportunity or a product—and when they get a "No", they freeze up. They turn that "No" into a failure.

That type of thinking will make failure your enemy. As a result, you will think too small, aim too low, and quit too soon. You'll also guarantee that success will remain a stranger to you.

When I was young, I read a book entitled, *The Greatest Salesman in the World* by Og Mandino. He wrote, "Whenever you make a mistake or get knocked down by life, don't look back at it too long. Mistakes are life's way of teaching you. Your capacity for occasional blunders is inseparable from your capacity to reach your goals. No one wins them all, and your failures, when they happen, are just part of your growth. Shake off your blunders. How will you know your limits without an occasional failure? Never quit. Your turn will come."

Those words changed my perspective about failure. It became my friend and no longer was my enemy. I realized that if I didn't succeed at first, then I was

among the world's greatest achievers! In Network Mark
the-best get many, many "No's" in their business lifetim
to view those "No's" as one more step toward a "Yes!" Tl
friend.

How do you know when failure is your friend?

When you value the lessons it teaches you.

Don't count your losses—count your lessons! Whenever a person shares with me their disappointments and losses, I always ask "What did you learn?"

That's because when I look at my failures it's hard to call them failures. I've learned so much from each one and the growth from those lessons made me better for the next opportunity. That's the power of perspective: with the right perspective of failure, you discover that failure is inevitable, learning is optional, and growth is possible!

But only if failure is your friend.

If you dwell on the losses, failure will be your enemy. If you think about the lessons, failure will be your friend.

The following words help me keep a positive perspective about failure:

WHEN IT LOOKS LIKE I HAVE FAILED

Lord, are You trying to tell me something? For...

Failure does not mean I'm a failure;

It does mean I have not yet succeeded.

Failure does not mean I have accomplished nothing;

It does mean I have learned something.

Failure does not mean I have been a fool;

It does mean I had enough faith to experiment.

Failure does not mean I've been disgraced;

It does mean I dared to try.

Failure does not mean I don't have it;

It does mean I have to do something in a different way.

Failure does not mean I am inferior;

It does mean I am not perfect.

Failure does not mean I've wasted my life;

It does mean I have an excuse to start over again.

Failure does not mean I should give up;

It does mean I must try harder.

Failure does not mean I'll never make it;

It does mean I need more patience.

Failure does not mean You have abandoned me;

It does mean You mush have a better idea. Amen.

8. OTHERS ARE GROWING.

I experienced a significant challenge with the first organization I joined. They weren't growing! The people were content with being average and the organization was average...but I didn't want to be average! Birds of a feather flock together and I wasn't flocking, so I finally decided to leave my stagnant environment and go to a growing one.

How did I know I upgraded my choice?

I found people who desired to grow themselves like I did. Oh, happy day!

I quickly discovered that growth is the great separator between those who succeed and those who do not. That will also be your discovery as you join your Network Marketing team, and why it's so important to choose your team based on the following growth criteria. You will benefit greatly by being surrounded by others who are ...

- Outgrowing yesterday and growing into tomorrow.
- Outgrowing old expectations and growing into new expectations.
- Outgrowing past wins and growing into new victories.
- Outgrowing average relationships and growing into growing relationships.
- Outgrowing what was and growing into what could be.
- Outgrowing their old selves and growing into their new selves!

Growth's highest reward is not what you get from it, but what you become because of it. You will become bigger on the inside than you are on the outside. The result? You will build yourself and your business because you thrive in a growing environment.

9. PEOPLE DESIRE CHANGE.

Here's the good news: it only takes one person to change your life...*you!*

And here's the bad news: you have to make those changes.

Have you ever been like me? I used to say, "I sure hope things will change." Then I discovered that the only way things are going to change is when I change!

In a Network Marketing growth environment, people desire change either out of desperation or inspiration. Both at times have motivated me to make personal changes. Here's some insight on how they are different:

> ***Desperation Changes:*** People sometimes change when they hurt enough that they have to. Their motivation is to leave something or someone that they greatly dislike. They are looking for "the greener grass on the other side." They are looking to trade their pain in life for a purpose. Many people become a part of Network Marketing because they desire a better life for themselves.
>
> ***Inspiration Changes:*** People often change because they have discovered another way to live that inspires their life. Their motivation is to go to something or someone who inspires them.

Albert Schweitzer wrote, "Sometimes our light goes out, but is blown into flame by another human being. Each of us owes deepest thanks to those who have rekindled this light."

Millions of people would give credit to Network Marketing for reigniting their personal flame. They became alive again when they entered this growth environment. They were inspired to change which resulted into a better life for them.

10. GROWTH IS MODELED AND EXPECTED.

People do what people see. Ben Franklin said, "Tell me and I forget. Teach me and I remember. Involve me and I learn." I would add to his quote, "Show me and I will follow; empower me and I will grow." Most things in life are more "caught than taught: Get ready to play "catch!"

Let's review the growth environment that this network marketing organization will provide for you. Place a check mark beside the areas that motivate you to develop yourself.

This Organization Provides a Place Where ...

_______ Others are ahead of me.
_______ I am continually challenged.
_______ My focus is forward.
_______ The atmosphere is affirming.
_______ I am out of my comfort zone.
_______ I wake up excited.
_______ Failure is not my enemy.
_______ Others are growing.
_______ I desire to change.
_______ Growth is modeled for me and expected of me.

As you finish this chapter, I am excited for you because I know what lies ahead! You're about to embark on one of the most exciting and profitable journeys you'll ever undertake—and it will all be thanks to your choice to grow as a person. It won't always be easy, and it won't always be fun, but it will always produce a return on your investment. And it will make you a better person in the end.

EXERCISE: A • C • T

Let me share with you an exercise I have used for over 30 years. I have discovered that the greatest benefit after hearing a lecture or reading a book are my action steps. I always ask myself "What do I need to apply or change in my life or teach someone else?"

I call this exercise A C T. When reading each chapter, I would suggest that you write an A, C or T in the margin to make you aware of the things that you want to act upon.

Apply - What is the most important lesson I need to Apply to myself in this Chapter on Growth Matters?

____

____

____

____

____

Change - What is the most important thing I need to Change in my life from this Chapter on Growth Matters?

____

____

____

____

____

Teach - What is the most important thing I need to Teach others from this Chapter on Growth Matters?

____

____

____

____

____

RECOMMENDED READING:

Self-Improvement 101 - John C. Maxwell

The 15 Invaluable Laws of Growth – John C. Maxwell

Put Your Dream to The Test – John C. Maxwell

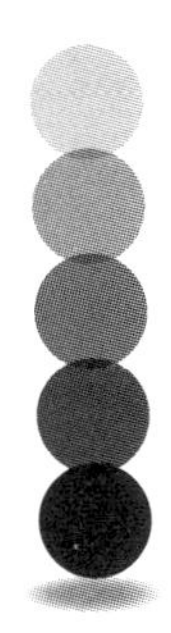

POWER #2
CONNECTION

As a 12-year-old I began walking down what I now call, "the people path." When I was in the 7th grade I read the book *How to Win Friends and Influence People* by Dale Carnegie. As I turned the pages, I began to underline many of his thoughts about relationships. Decades later, there are still plenty of thoughts from that book that help me as leader. Here are a few that I find valuable, because I believe they will benefit you, too:

- "The rare individual who unselfishly tries to serve others has an enormous advantage."
- "A person's name is the sweetest and most important sound in any language."
- "Success in dealing with people depends on a sympathetic grasp of the other person's viewpoint."
- "To be interesting, be interested."
- "Talk to someone about themselves and they'll listen for hours."

Dale Carnegie awakened within me the desire to understand and connect with others. Every year through high school I re-read his book. On my bookshelves is a section where I have special books that have impacted my life. Today, as I sit in my office writing these words to you, I look over and see that book. It makes me smile.

I was so impacted by Carnegie's work that in 2004 I attempted to write my own book about relationships. It's called *Winning with People*, and its thesis is simple: *People can usually trace their successes and failures to the relationships in their lives.* I know that's certainly been the case for me in my career, and I believe the same is true for you—especially in the Network Marketing industry!

That's because Network Marketing is all about people—finding, connecting, and developing relationships with others is the key to industry success. The better you are at connecting with others, the greater your opportunities for sustained success in your career.

Because connecting with others is such a crucial skill set to have, I'd like to share a few of my people principles with you. Here are just a few of the 25 principles I outline in *Winning with People:*

- ***The Lens Principle:*** Who We Are Determines How We See Others.

- ***The Hammer Principle:*** Never Use a Hammer to Swat a Fly Off of Someone's Forehead.
- ***The Elevator Principle:*** We Can Lift People Up or Take People Down in Our Relationships.
- ***The Big Picture Principle:*** The Entire Population of the World - With One Minor Exception- Is Composed of Others.
- ***The Charisma Principle:*** People Are Interested in the Person Who is Interested in Them.
- ***The Bedrock Principle:*** Trust is the Foundation of Any Relationship.
- ***The "Bob" Principle:*** When Bob Has a Problem with Everyone, Bob is Usually the Problem.
- ***The Gardening Principle:*** All Relationships Need Cultivation.
- ***The Patience Principle:*** The Journey with Others is Slower Than the Journey Alone.
- ***The High Road Principle:*** We Go to a Higher Level When We Treat Others Better Than They Treat Us.
- ***The Boomerang Principle:*** When We Help Others, We Help Ourselves.
- ***The Partnership Principle:*** Working Together Increases the Odds of Winning Together.

Okay, I got carried away. I gave you almost half of the people principles in my book!

Why would I do that? Because I want you to have, "People Success" in your life. Nothing will help you do well in life more than your ability to positively connect with others. NOTHING!

I love the story of Pam, who is a Network Marketer on the East Coast. When Pam was just starting out in the business, she had no idea how to connect with people. But she read everything she could on how to connect with people—concepts like the value of listening, how to ask good questions, practicing open body language, and how to spot cues that others are interested in connecting. Pam knew connection would help her succeed.

This is where the story gets good.

Pam was at a party where she was supposed to present. She expected a fairly large crowd, but instead, was greeted by one guest. At first, she was disappointed, but she quickly realized that if she could make an impact on one person, it was still worth it. At the end of her presentation, she pulled a chair next to the man and asked, "Will you share with me what you're passionate about?"

The man opened up about his passion for making a difference in the lives of other people, and Pam was able to tell him about the hundreds of people Network Marketing had allowed her to influence. The conversation deepened, and as the man poured out his troubles, including a devastating financial loss, Pam leaned into the moment, giving him the space to be honest about himself and his dreams.

After listening and talking with him for a long time, Pam sat up, looked him dead in the eye and asked, "Do you trust me?"

"Yes, I do," he replied.

Pam asked a second question: "Are you coachable?"

"Yes, I am," came the answer.

Pam said, "If you will be coachable, and listen to the things that I teach you, I promise you we will get back for you everything that you've lost."

The man joined her team on the spot. And as Pam coached him, he began to rebuild his life—ultimately building a team of 15,000 people! Not only was the man able to recover from his financial losses, but he and his wife were able to make enough money that they could cover the medical expenses for her father's cancer treatments when became ill years later.

The power of connection is the power to make someone else feel heard, to make them feel that they matter. But connection also creates opportunities to help someone grow and succeed. Pam's story is a reminder that making time to connect with people, and learning to do it well, is a power every successful Network Marketer needs.

The rest of this chapter will help you develop what I call "Connecting Practices." There are many effective ways to connect with people. As you incorporate more and more of these practices into your daily work, you will see steady improvement in your people skills as well as growth in your Network Marketing business.

CONNECTING PRACTICES

1. PRACTICE THE VALUE OF CONNECTING WITH PEOPLE.

As a kid in junior high I began to see the value of developing my people skills. That "people path" I have been traveling has served me very well. My biggest take away from this journey is this:

> **Almost everything we become and accomplish in life is with and through people. Therefore, the ability to connect and create relationships with others is the most important skill that we can learn.**

With all the emphasis our culture places on education, you might think that knowledge is the greatest asset to build your business. However the Carnegie Foundation discovered that *relational skills* are far more important if you want a bright future. Their study found that only 15% of a person's success is determined by job knowledge and technical skills, while 85% is determined by an individual's attitude and ability to relate to people.

Charles Schulz, the creator of the *Peanuts* comic strip, developed an interesting exercise to help drive home the importance of relationships in our daily lives. See how well you do on his little quiz:

1. Name three of the wealthiest people in the world.
2. Name three of the last five Heisman trophy winners.
3. Name three of the people who have won the Nobel or Pulitzer Prize.
4. Name three of the last five Academy Award winners for best actress.
5. Name three of the last five Grammy winners for Album of the Year.

How did you do? Unless you're a trivia whiz, chances are you struggled with one or two of those categories. Regardless of your score, however, the point is that few of us remember the headlines of yesterday. The answers to each of those questions aren't second-rate achievers; they were and are the best in their fields! But the applause dies. Awards tarnish. Achievements are forgotten.

Here's another quiz. See how you do on this one:

1. List three teachers who aided your journey through school.
2. Name three friends who have helped you through a difficult time.
3. Name three people who have taught you something worthwhile.
4. Think of three people who have made you feel appreciated and special!
5. Think of three people you enjoy spending time with.

Was this quiz easier for you? Of course! You likely had little trouble thinking of names for most—if not all—of these questions because of the impact each person made on your life. You tend to remember more of the people who made a mark on *you* than the people who made a mark on *history*.

People like the folks who introduced you to Network Marketing.

The lesson in all of this? The people who make a difference in your life are not the ones with the most money, most credentials, or the most awards. They simply are the people who have connected with you, invested in you, and care the most about you.

It's become cliché, but it's still true: *people don't care how much you know until they know how much you care.*

2. PRACTICE VALUING PEOPLE AND LET THEM KNOW IT.

In his book, *Start with Why*, author Simon Sinek says, "People don't buy what you do. They buy why you do it."

The *why* is all about motives, and good motives are essential when connecting with others. Genuinely valuing other people is a foundational motive that keeps all other motives pure when relating to people. I often say that it's wonderful when the people believe in their leader, but it's more wonderful when the leader believes in the people!

The people who introduced you to this business obviously believe in you. They have placed a "10" on your head. They chose to invest in you and your potential because they are motivated to see you succeed. They see you as you could be, not just as you are.

You have an opportunity to do the same thing for others. There are two specific things you can do to value people and let them know it.

First, let them know that you need them—because you can't be successful without them! In my book, *The 17 Indisputable Laws of Teamwork,* the Law of Significance says, "One Is Too Small a Number to Achieve Greatness." Those around you complement and complete you. When they do that, make sure to continually let them know it.

Second, compliment people in front of other people—especially their family and friends. Praise people in private and you add; praise people in public and you multiply. Every person has a desire to be recognized for the good things that they do, so don't hold back on genuine praise.

Author Jim Rohn said, "Start with where the people are before you try to take them where you want them to go." Do exactly that. Start with valuing people and then help them become even more valuable.

3. Practice Adding Value to People Every Day.

What you are about to read has the potential to change your life. I make the following part of my daily routine, and I promise you this connection practice brings a significant return on investment.

These are the five things you can do every day that will help you connect with people and increase your influence with them. These things are simple yet powerful, and you can do them starting right now. You should write these five things down in your journal, type them into a note on your phone, or take a picture that you can reference from time to time. They will become the foundation for connecting with others daily.

EVERY DAY I WILL

1. Value People. This perspective will bring the best out of you and others.

2. Think of Ways to Add Value to People. Every Morning look at your schedule and ask yourself, "Who will I see and how can I add value to them?"

3. Look for Ways to Add Value to People. Who we are determines what we see. If you are a plus in your relationships, you will find positive things to say and do that will add value.

4. Do Things That Add Value to People. Every evening, look at your day and reflect on it. Ask yourself: "Did I add value to someone? Who was it? What did I do?" Evaluate your day based on the seeds you sow, not the harvest you reap.

5. Encourage Others to Add Value to People. As you do those four things consistently you will encourage others to do the same. Before long, your entire team will be intentionally adding value to others.

4. Practice Walking Slowly Through the Crowd.

In Latin, the root word for communication is "communis," which is literally translated as common. I love this little tidbit because it reinforces something I've taught about communication for years. Namely, you connect with people when you find common ground with them.

The best way to find common ground with others is to go where they are and walk slowly through the crowd. I learned this as a young man when I watched my father, Melvin, take time to interact with students at the college where he served as president. Dad would walk through the quad and take time to talk to as many students as he could. He made time to give time to the people who needed—and desired—it most.

Network Marketing is a people business. There will always be a crowd of some sort that you will encounter, and walking slowly through the crowd means:

- Being approachable.
- Making time to connect with people.

- Observing best practices of others.
- Asking questions.
- Listening to others.
- Identifying needs and meeting them.
- Serving those around you.
- Bringing out the best in others

Many years ago, I was in the lobby of our office talking with six team members. One of my young staff members entered the lobby and walked right past us without saying anything. I excused myself and followed him to his office.

Sitting down across from his desk, I said to him, “You must be in a hurry.”

“Yes, I am,” he said. “I have a lot of work to do today.”

In a fatherly way, I replied, “You passed your work in the lobby.”

He looked at me confused, so I continued.

“When you came in, you breezed by your teammates without even saying hello,” I said. “We are in the people business, and you just passed your business.”

He learned a valuable lesson in that moment, and he quickly adopted the practice of walking slowly through the crowd—something he continues to this day.

Business author Jeffrey Gitomer shared a powerful insight on his blog when he wrote:

> “Here’s the rock, paper, scissors game of connecting:
> Relationship is more powerful than price.
> Relationship is more powerful than delivery.
> Relationship is more powerful than quality.
> Relationship is more powerful than service.”

My friend, Jimmy Blanchard, a very successful business builder, says, “The common thread in great organizations is valuing and respecting people.” Instead of putting *others* in their place, put *yourself* in their place. When you’re there, others will know that you cared enough to move toward them instead of expecting them to move toward you. Walking close to people helps you quickly recognize their strengths and weaknesses.

There's a classic Peanuts comic strip that sums up what it means to walk slowly through the crowd. In the strip, Lucy says to Snoopy, "There are times when you really bug me, but I must admit there are also times when I feel like giving you a big hug."

Snoopy replies, "That's the way I am . . .huggable and buggable."

We all have some Snoopy in us. Walking slowly through the crowd lets us know we're not alone.

5. Practice Asking Questions and Listening Well.

Recently, I sat down with the coaching consultants of The John Maxwell Team. It had been a year since our last meeting, and I was excited to spend time with them. At the beginning of the meeting they expected me to start talking—so they were surprised when I said that I wanted to listen first, ask some questions, and *then* talk.

Why did I do that?

Because asking questions and listening is a great channel for connection.

Management expert Peter Drucker once said, "My greatest strength as a consultant is to be ignorant and ask some questions." Quality questions create a quality life. Successful people ask better questions and as a result, get better answers. Questions are keys to unlock doors to better relationships.

People connect when they understand, but they commit when they feel understood. That only happens when we ask questions and listen. Asking questions helps you gain clarity on the other person's thoughts and ideas—and communicates to them that you value those thoughts and ideas! Questions build connection.

As a builder and a leader in business I've discovered that before I can set things right, I need to see things right. Likewise, instead of trying to impress others and be interesting to them, I should be impressed with and interested in them. That only happens if I listen. Listening builds trust.

The ability to ask good questions and listen well is the foundation to building positive relationships with others and is a vital skill in communicating effectively. You need to intentionally cultivate both habits if you want to ensure your success in your industry.

Here is what good questions and great listening allow successful Network Marketers do:

1. Show Respect. Edgar Watson Howe once joked, "No man would listen to you talk if he didn't know it was his turn next." Unfortunately, that accurately describes the way too many people approach communication - they're too busy waiting for their turn to really listen to others.
2. Build Relationships. By becoming a good listener, you are able to connect with others on more levels and develop stronger, deeper relationships because you are meeting a need.
3. Increase Knowledge. It's amazing how much you can learn about your friends and family, your job, the organization you work in, and yourself when you decide to really listen to others.
4. Generate Ideas. If you give people opportunities to share their thoughts, and you listen with an open mind, there will always be a flow of new ideas. And even if you hear ideas that won't work, just listening to them can often spark other creative thoughts in you and others.
5. Build Loyalty. Practicing good listening skills draws people to you. Everyone loves a good listener and is attracted to him or her. And if you consistently listen to others, valuing them and what they have to offer, they are likely to develop a strong loyalty to you, even if your relationships with them are formal or informal.

Allow me to encourage you. As a young leader I did not ask questions or listen well. I had "agenda anxiety", which was the result of thinking that what I needed to say was more important than what others wanted to say to me.

Fortunately, I was confronted by my staff and challenged to listen more and better. Changing my bad habit wasn't easy, but after much effort on my part, and with help from my team, I changed.

Today I know that each person I meet has something to teach me if I ask questions and listen. The same can be true for you.

6. Practice Discovering and Developing Your Connecting Strengths.

Looking back on my early days of building a business, I wish I would have known then what I will now share with you. It was a pivotal discovery for me, and I believe it can have a similar impact on you.

My discovery was this: if you use your natural strengths to connect with others, you will experience relational success. In other words, take the positive strengths of who you are and use them to connect with people where they are.

Reading the book *Strength Finders* by Tom Rath was life changing for me. One of my strengths was "Woo," which means I have charisma. Charisma is simple way of saying that people are drawn to me because I am drawn to people.

After reading about that strength, I began to ask myself, w*hat is the make-up of my Woo?* Seeking the answer to that question led me to list out my connecting strengths. These strengths are unique to me, so I only share these with you to illustrate what connecting strengths are, and prompt you to find yours.

My six connecting strengths are...

- ***Humor*** **-** I enjoy people and find humor in almost anything. Therefore, I use it to often connect with others. Laughing is a positive way to connect.
- ***Authenticity*** **-** I'm comfortable with myself and therefore talk easily about my strengths and weaknesses. My openness to others makes me approachable and reachable.
- ***Confidence*** **-** I naturally feel good about myself and others. This allows people to feel secure with me and venture outside of their comfort zone.
- ***Hope*** **-** I love to encourage others because of my belief in their potential. My positive attitude gives positive vibes.
- ***Passion*** **-** I love what I do and love the people I do life with. Passion is the great energizer. When others ask me how I can keep the pace of my schedule, I laugh and say, "High energy - low IQ!"
- ***Simplicity*** **-** "My name is John and I'm your friend." I've said that phrase thousands of times. It describes me—I'm a communicator who makes complicated things simple. I'm not an intellectual. I have to simplify life myself, and I do it for others.

Those are my connecting strengths. What are yours? Discuss this with your friends and let them help you discover your connecting strengths. Then develop them. When you are at your best, is when you best connect with people.

*7. **Practice and Identify the 7 Motivations of People.***

Often the phrase "working hard" and "working smart" are positioned as either/or. That does not have to be the case! When we understand what motivates ourselves and others, we can work hard and smart simultaneously.

To that end, I've compiled a list of the 7 Motivations of People, and I'm sharing it to position you well for winning with people.

The 7 Motivations of People

1.) Purpose: People Want to Do What They Were Created to Do.

Clare Boothe Luce was one of the first women to serve in the United States Congress. Right after John F. Kennedy was elected President, she offered him this advice, "A great man is one sentence." She then illustrated her point.

She summarized Abraham Lincoln with, "He preserved the Union and freed the slaves."

Franklin Roosevelt's sentence was, "He lifted us out of the Great Depression and helped us win the World War."

Luce looked at President Kennedy and asked, "So what is your one sentence?"

Network Marketing organizations give you the opportunity to find your "one sentence." You are now a part of a culture that encourages personal growth and your possibilities.

This uplifting environment will push you to ask yourself, "What is my one sentence?"—and then applaud you as you discover it.

2.) Autonomy: People Want to Have Freedom to Control Their Lives.

Cornell University studied 320 small businesses. Half allowed their people autonomy. These businesses grew four times the rate of the more control-oriented companies.

My speaking and travels take me to many countries and cultures. Some of which are highly authoritarian and controlling. There is a lack of energy and creativity within those environments. I always feel that when I am in those environments that the people would do so much better if they were allowed to have a little more control of their destiny's.

However, when I speak at Network Marketing events, it is a breath of fresh air. The people attend because they want to be there. They have the freedom to have some control their business, determine their future, make their own decisions and pursue their dreams.

In my book, *Put Your Dream to the Test*, I write about The Ownership Question, which asks, "Is my dream really my dream?" Notice the difference between your dream and someone else's dream for you:

When It's Your Dream	When It's Someone's Dream For You
It will provide wings to your spirit.	It will be a weight on your shoulder.
It will fire you up.	It will drain your energy.
It will fulfill you.	It will fulfill others.
You will want to do it.	Others will want you to do it.

When the dream is right for you and you are right for the dream, the two cannot be separated from each other!

3.) Relationships: People Want to Do Things with Others.

I'm often asked what motivates me to keep on working. My fun answer is, "High energy and low IQ." However, my real answer is two-fold: My Purpose: I want to add value to leaders who multiply value to other, and My Relationships: I love the people that work with me and the work we are doing together.

In my book *Winning with People* I write about The Friendship Principle- "All things being equal people will work with people they like; all things not being equal, they still will." That is so true! We like to work with people we like.

As I've said elsewhere in this book, Network Marketing is a people business. It allows you to build your team with your friends and others who want to help others and themselves live a better life. There is a "family feeling" in these organizations. Doing something that you love with people you love is very motivating.

4.) Progress: People Want to Experience Personal and Professional Growth.

Network Marketing has no equal when it comes to helping people experience personal and professional growth. In my opinion, they are the very best at helping people become their very best. If you are inspired by the possibility of finding and reaching your potential, then you have found the right place!

Progress is a high motivation factor in my life. Can I give you a "progress thought" that will help you? Here it is:

It wasn't the big hit, the home run, the magic answer that suddenly turned my dreams into reality.

My big hit never came without a lot of daily little hits. My friend, there is no secret to success, no rocket ride to the top, no silver bullet to achieving your dreams. There is just steady, consistent, determined progress forward. You must follow the correct pathway to make progress and realize your deepest desires.

The good news is the pathway is as obvious as it is challenging: every day do the things that are essential to building your business.

EVERY.

DAY.

Don't settle for a good day followed by a string of mediocre days. Make each day your masterpiece. Consistency compounds! Every day you spend doing what's essential will someday give you your dream.

5.) Mastery: People Want to Excel in Their Skill.

Throughout history, the word "excellence" is often used as a title of honor. It derives from the word "excel," which means to go beyond average. Going beyond average is the challenge of mastery. I love what NBA Hall of Famer Pat Riley once wrote: "Excellence is the gradual result of always striving to be better."

That means excellence only happens as we consistently exceed expectations.

An early temptation of mine was to "wing it" instead of "work at it." I realized that my giftedness would allow me to get by with less and not give the effort required for most people.

After a few months of considering this temptation I concluded that mindset was not for me. I wrote this promise to myself: "I will not take short cuts nor will I cut corners. Even if others would say I could, my passion would tell me that I couldn't."

My journey towards mastery began when I strived to exceed the expectations every day in my business, and the same is true for you. Your Network Marketing organization has no high achievers who love average. They are motivated to do their best everyday so they could become the best someday.

Excellence is not an exception. It is a prevailing attitude.

6.) Recognition: People Want People to Recognize Their Accomplishments.

> "A gossip is one who talks to you about other people.
> A bore is one who talks to you about himself.
> A brilliant conversationalist is one who talks to you about yourself."
> -William King

The desire to be recognized and praised is within all of us. Psychologist Henry H. Goddard conducted a study of energy levels in children using an instrument he called the "ergograph," and his findings were fascinating.

He discovered that when children were given a word of praise, the ergograph showed an immediate surge of physical energy. When the children were criticized, the ergograph showed that their physical energy took a sudden nose dive.

I have been a part of several recognition events for multiple Network Marketing organizations. The auditorium is usually filled with energy as people walk across the stage and are recognized for their accomplishments. Progress is applauded. Growth is appreciated. People are valued...and motivation is experienced. People in the audience are often saying to themselves, "I am going to work hard and soon walk across that stage!"

How do I know?

Because the people who walk across those stages once were sitting in the audience themselves! I've heard the stories of several of the Ambassadors, and they've all shared about the motivation they derived from hearing their name called in recognition. A personal achievement made public instantly and dramatically increases in value.

7.) Money: People Want to Be Financially Secure.

This is last on *my* list of people motivators, but it is *first* on most people's list. I can understand—when you don't have financial security, wanting financial security is a worthy goal.

While I still believe that money isn't everything, money can get you financial freedom—and that provides you options. But fair warning: this motivator is more extrinsic than the others. There is a downside that comes with it if money is your only motivation.

Researchers at Rochester University conducted a two-year study on life goals. They found that those with extrinsic goals, such desiring wealth, had the same level of self-esteem over the two years of the study as participants with intrinsic goals. The catch was, extrinsically motivated participants had a much higher level of stress.

Those with intrinsic goals, such as learning, growth and helping others, had higher levels of satisfaction and lower anxiety.

My observation: Money is a powerful motivator until you have enough to give you what you want. Then its "pull" begins to lessen in your life.

My intent in sharing with you the 7 Motivations of People is to help you connect with yourself and with others. Once you understand these different motivations, it allows you to lead others and yourself uniquely.

In fact, do you know what I discovered about these 7 Motivators as I evaluated this list?

I realized all 7 motivated me!

My conclusion?

More motivations mean more discipline for the journey! The more ways you are motivated, the higher the odds that you will remain inspired while building your Network Marketing business.

PRACTICES OF CONNECTING - EVALUATION

Evaluate yourself on how well you're leveraging Connection with others. On a scale from 1 to 5 (where 1 is very low and 5 is very high) place a number beside each practice of Connection that you're likely to use daily.

_____ Practice the Value of Connecting with People.
_____ Practice Valuing People and Let Them Know It.
_____ Practice Adding Value to People... EVERYDAY!
_____ Practice Walking Slowly Through the Crowd.
_____ Practice Asking Questions and Listening Well.
_____ Practice Discovering and Developing Your Connecting Strengths.
_____ Practice and Identify the 7 Motivations of People.

EXERCISE: A • C • T

Apply - What is the most important lesson I need to Apply to myself in this Chapter on Connecting Matters?

____
____
____
____
____

Change - What is the most important thing I need to Change in my life from this Chapter on Connecting Matters?

____
____
____
____
____

Teach - What is the most important thing I need to Teach others from this Chapter on Connecting Matters?

____

____

____

____

____

RECOMMENDED READING:

Winning with People - John C. Maxwell

25 Ways to Win with People - John C. Maxwell

Everyone Communicates, Few Connect – John C. Maxwell

POWER #3
MINDSET

I see it happen all the time. Two people join a Network Marketing organization, with the same opportunity, at the same time, but their results are different. One succeeds and the other does not.

What happened? What was the difference between these two people?

It was their mindsets. Your mindset is the foundation of your life, and it carries into the process of building your business. Without a good one, your life and business will crumble and collapse when the storms inevitably come.

My friend, Callie, has a great story about the power of mindset, and she shared it with me to help you understand how important this power truly is:

> When I first began my business, I went to one of my closest girlfriends and told her what I was starting. She'd recently come through a very difficult time and was just trying to survive, but I knew her potential, and I knew if she could step into the right mindset, her life would transform.
>
> We launched her business and got off to a great start, but shortly after it slowed down, she was still struggling to pay her bills as her business wasn't able to fully support her. I wanted her to see the potential so bad, but it just wasn't happening.
>
> She was really frustrated, but then something happened: she attended a personal development event.
>
> When she got back, it was as if a light bulb had come on. She was ready to step into her potential and it dramatically transformed her life. She changed how she was building her business and over time replaced her income, quit her other jobs and could finally be at home with her kids. She hasn't looked back since—her mindset is forever changed!

I love that story because it shows exactly how mindset unlocks opportunity. What we think and how we think makes such a difference in what we do and how we do it!

I often say, "If I could do one thing to help any person succeed in life, it would be to help them think successfully." My father helped me as a boy to develop a mindset that would allow me to reach my potential. He would often quote this Proverb to me, "As you think in your heart, so you will be." He realized that my thinking would determine who I became. He placed good books in my hands and paid me to read them.

Two of these books made a great impression on my thinking mindset: *The Magic of Thinking Big*, by David J. Schwartz, and *How to Win Friends and Influence People*, by Dale Carnegie, which I wrote about in the last chapter. Those books were full of powerful ideas for my young mind, and I want to share a quote from each that underscores the importance of thinking:

"Where success is concerned, people are not measured in inches, or pounds, or college degrees, or family background; they are measured by the size of their thinking."
~David J. Schwartz, *The Magic of Thinking Big*

"The biggest lesson I have ever learned is the stupendous importance of what we think. If I knew what you think, I would know what you are, for your thoughts make you what you are; by changing our thoughts we can change our lives."
~Dale Carnegie, *How to Win Friends and Influence People*

Thinking was such a foundational tool for me that the first book I wrote was entitled, *Think on These Things*. I wanted to provide my own tool for helping others develop a thinking mindset. No matter who you are, you are exactly where your thoughts have brought you, and tomorrow you will be where your thoughts take you.

Thinking is so critical to your success that before I share how to develop a proper mindset, I need to share my favorite illustration of why mindset is important. It's a story of someone who just didn't think.

Larry Walters wanted to fly. He was a risk taker. He got an idea one day while sitting outdoors in his extremely comfortable lawn chair. He purchased 45 weather balloons from an army-navy surplus store, tied them to his tethered lawn chair dubbed "The Inspiration One" and filled the four-foot diameter balloons with helium.

Then he strapped himself into his lawn chair with some sandwiches, Miller Lite beer and a pellet gun. Larry's plan was to sever the anchor and lazily float up to a height of about 30 feet above his backyard where he would enjoy a few hours of flight before coming back down.

He figured he'd pop a few brews, then pop a few balloons when it was time to descend, and gradually lose altitude; but things did not work out quite as Larry had planned.

When his friends cut the cord anchoring the lawn chair to his Jeep, he did not float lazily up to 30 feet. Instead, he streaked into the LA skies as if shot from a cannon, pulled by the lift of 45 helium balloons holding 33 cubic feet of helium each. He didn't level off at a hundred feet; he didn't level off at a thousand feet.

After climbing and climbing, he leveled off at 16,000 feet.

At that height he felt he couldn't risk shooting any of the balloons lest he unbalance the load and find himself in real trouble. So, he stayed there, drifting with his sandwiches and beer for several hours while he considered his options. At one point he crossed the primary approach corridor of Los Angeles LAX airspace, as airline pilots radioed in incredulous reports of this strange sight.

Eventually Larry gathered the nerve to shoot a few balloons and slowly descended through the night sky. The tethers hanging from his chair got tangled up and caught in a power line, blacking out a Long Beach neighborhood for 20 minutes. But it allowed Larry to climb to safety, where he was arrested by waiting members of the Los Angeles Police Department.

As he was led away in handcuffs, a reporter dispatched to cover the daring rescue asked him why he had done it.

Larry replied nonchalantly, “A man can't just sit around.”

Hilarious story! I told this story one time and a guy who flew for Delta came up to me afterwards.

He had flown that day and he said he was one of the ones that radioed into the tower, and every radio report from every pilot, he said, began with the same phrase – “You're not going to believe this...”

THE RIGHT MINDSET

Sometimes, it's difficult to believe what people are thinking. Like Larry, for some folks, a little bit of thought could go a long way. So let's take a moment to establish the two reasons why the right mindset toward thinking is essential for your success.

1. The Right Mindset Creates a Foundation for Good Results.

Good thoughts and actions usually produce good results. Front-end thinking is the foundation for everything that comes afterward. Some people like to say all is well that *ends* well, but I believe that all is well that *begins* well.

Ask these people how important a proper mindset is in the beginning:

- The coach before the players take the field.
- The surgeon before the patient has surgery.
- The teacher before the student takes the test.
- The mentor before a person becomes a Network Marketer.

2. The Right Mindset Increases Your Potential.

Harvard psychologist William James said, "The greatest discovery of my generation is that a human being can alter his life by altering his attitudes of mind." You change your life when you change how you think.

In other words, your potential is determined by your mindset.

Take a look at the following list that highlights the difference between average people and successful people in the Network Marketing industry:

AVERAGE PEOPLE	SUCCESSFUL PEOPLE
See Only Their Point of View	See the Big Picture
Go in Too Many Directions	Focus on the Main Thing
Are Stuck Inside Their Box	Explore Options and Innovate
Hope for the Best	Face the Facts and Build Upon Them
Let Life Happen to Them	Proactively Plan Their Lives
Allow Circumstances to Limit Them	See Possibilities Everywhere
Don't Learn from Mistakes	Stop, Reflect, and Learn Daily
Follow the Crowd	Challenge Popular "Wisdom"
Try to Make It on Their Own	Know Success Requires a Team
Focus on Helping Themselves	Benefit from Adding Value to Others
Try When They Feel Like It	Try When They Don't Feel Like It

3. The Right Mindset Is Intentional.

Intentional *thinking* precedes intentional *living*. The intentional life is deliberate, consistent and willful. The unintentional life is passive, inconsistent and disappointing. Sadly, most people accept their life instead of living it! They get the left-overs instead of the main course.

Let me ask you a question: do you spend today preparing for tomorrow or repairing from yesterday? People with the right mindset are intentional and prepare. People with the wrong mindset are unintentional and repair.

One of the greatest gaps in life is between sounding good and doing good. Some people are always "getting ready to get ready." Intentional living is the great dividing line between words and results. My mentor, John Wooden, would often say to me, "John, don't tell me what you are going to do, show me."

I have a question for you—*would your life improve if you turned good intention into good action?* I think we both know the answer to that question.

DEVELOPING AN INTENTIONAL MINDSET

Many of my successful Network Marketing friends would say intentional thinking was the first step to their business growing, and it's my experience that a few small steps in the right direction became some of the biggest steps in my life.

You can have the better life you're longing for, if you'll choose it. These mindset choices that you are about to read will help turn your desire into action, turn someday into today, turn occasional into continual, and turn dreaming into doing. Let's get started.

1. I Choose to Be Realistic.

Anyone who's ever been lost in a mall or a theme park knows the value of the "You Are Here" star on a map. You must know where you are before you can chart the course for where you want to go. That's why reality should be the foundation for the dream that you have. Reality is the difference between what we wish for, what we have and the changes we need to make to reach our desired destination. Take a moment and answer these questions:

- Where are you?
- Where do you want to be?
- What changes do you need to make?

When you can answer those questions, you have the outline for the reality you're facing. You can begin thinking realistically. There are three benefits to realistic thinking:

- **Realistic thinking is a catalyst for change.**
Hope is merely a state of mind, and while it is a positive place to be it is not enough to get you into action. People who rely on hope for their success rarely make change a high priority. If you have only hope, you imply that achievement and success are out of your hands. It's a matter of luck or chance. Why bother changing? Realistic thinking on the other hand, combined with intentional action, is what brings about change, results and ultimately success.

- **Realistic thinking gives you credibility.**
Often there is a gap between a person's words and actions. What I say I'm going to do is inspiring in the beginning, but it must soon be backed up with results. When that doesn't happen, I will have a credibility gap with others. Realistic thinking will not allow that to happen.

- **Realistic thinking brings your dream into reality.**
British novelist John Galsworthy wrote, "Idealism increases in direct proportion to one's distance from the problem." If you don't recognize the challenges of reaching your dream and don't face them, you will never achieve your heart's desire.

Realistic thinking is incredibly important when it comes to building a successful business in Network Marketing. Many people forget that when you start a business there is one essential requirement: work! Often, there is a false expectation that success happens over-night, and millions are made instantly. This is the furthest thing from the truth.

I have many friends who have been very successful in Network Marketing, and many of them more successful than traditional business owners, but that does not mean that it happened effortlessly. Like all things worthwhile, success takes time, energy and compounded efforts. You will be required to put in sweat equity. You will go through multiple cycles of success and failure. At times you will win, and at other times you will learn.

It saddens me when people in Network Marketing are fantasizers instead of dream builders. Look at how differently they approach achieving their dream:

FANTASIZERS...	DREAM BUILDERS...
Rely on luck.	Rely on discipline.
Focus on the destination.	Focus on the journey.
Cultivate unhealthy expectations.	Cultivate healthy discontent.
Minimize the value of work.	Maximize the work they do.
Look for excuses.	Lead to action.
Create inertia.	Generate momentum.
Breed isolation.	Promote teamwork.
Wait.	Initiate.
Avoid personal risks.	Embrace risk as necessary.
Make others responsible.	Make themselves responsible.

Football icon Rudy Ruettiger said, “Reality is the enemy of fantasies but not of our dreams.” I love that! Beginning with the expectation that you’ll experience challenges will help prevent you from becoming discouraged when you do.

In my book, *Put Your Dream to the Test*, I ask ten questions that you must answer to determine if your dream can come true. One of those is the Reality Question, which asks, “Am I depending on factors within my control to realize my dream?” Remember, the dream is free, but the journey isn’t. Realistic thinking helps you pay the price needed to achieve your dream.

2. I Choose to Be Coachable.

Lou Holtz was one of the greatest coaches in college football. He is known for helping his players reach their peak performance on the football field. We were having lunch one day and he said to me, “I’ve coached good players and I’ve coached bad players. I’m a better coach with good players.” We both laughed!

Then I asked, “What makes a good player?”

He responded, “Great skills and a coachable attitude.”

The etymology of the word *coach* comes from a Hungarian town called Kocs, which produced—you guessed it—coaches! Over time, the carriages (called *kocsi szeker)* gained popularity world-wide, and various languages adopted some form of the name: *kutsche* in German, *coche* in French, and the English word *coach*.

The point is, when you placed yourself into a coach, you knew that you would arrive at your desired destination. Coaches were synonymous for getting you to get where you want to go.

My friend Dianna Kokoszka, who has trained and coached thousands of people, has dug in on the power of coaching. Dianna says, "After taking a class, the average person has a 22 percent increase in performance. That same person who is coached will have an increase of 88 percent!"

There have been many mentors and coaches in my life, and all contributed to making me better. This much I know—I can go farther and faster with someone coaching me than I can on my own. The impact of good coaching also led to the creation of my successful coaching company which, after eleven years, is truly global in its influence.

What else have I learned about coaching?

It is impossible to maximize your potential in any area without it. You may be good. You may even be better than everyone else. But without someone mentoring you, you will never be as good as you *could* be. Self-evaluation is helpful, but evaluation with someone else is essential. The purpose of coaching is to improve both the person and the performance.

But even the best coach can't overcome a bad attitude. That's why, to maximize improvement of yourself and your performance, you need to have a coachable attitude.

I call this *teachability*. Teachability is when a person pairs a desire to grow with humility. Humility is essential for coaching, because it recognizes that you are a work in progress and need coaching to help you develop.

Maintaining teachability requires repeated long, hard looks in the mirror. You must constantly evaluate your effectiveness and develop new skills to meet the challenges of building your business. Teachability isn't afraid to ask, "Am I the bottleneck here?" and then make changes if the answer comes back "Yes."

In the Network Marketing industry, teachability shows up when people look at their previous track record and recognize that a history of repeated failures or bad experiences may reflect solely on them. It's seen when people who are not having the success they thought possible ask themselves if they are being coachable to the systems their company has in place.

In your Network Marketing organization, you have leaders who are successful. Go to them. Learn from them. Ask questions. Follow their example. Let them speak into your life. Seek feedback and constructive criticism. Systems are in place for you to duplicate. Learn the system and then do it. Principles are given to help you build your business. Practice them.

If you are still not having the level of success you know you are capable of, you need to check your teachability. You're ready to seek helpful direction after you can answer "Yes" to the following questions:

- "Do I have the desire to continually improve?"
- "Do I realize that I need the help of others?"
- "Do I want to be coached by others?"
- "Am I willing to make the necessary changes to improve?"
- "Do I easily give credit to those who help me?"
- "Do I desire feedback and make appropriate changes from it?"

Being coachable requires a commitment to grow in the context of your community by letting others speak into your life.

3. I Choose to Be Positive.

The thesis of my book *The Difference Maker* is, "Attitude isn't everything, but it is the one thing that can make a difference in your life."

Often, I am asked to identify the single most important aspect of a positive attitude. My answer: "Possessing a 'whatever it takes' mindset."

A "whatever it takes" mindset is simply a positive attitude with some "muscle" in it! Your Network Marketing organization is a gym that will help you develop the necessary muscle in your attitude.

The following should be your mindset workout...

(1) Disarm Your Helplessness.

"Whatever it takes" people aggressively pursue solutions. You never hear them say, "There's nothing I can do about it!" Those are the words of a victim's mindset. You develop muscle in your attitude when you believe there is always an answer and that you are a part of that answer. This spirit causes you to stand while others sit, move forward while others wait and find answers when others only have questions. You disown your helplessness when you say to yourself and others, "I can make a difference!"

(2) Answer the Hard Questions.

- "What do I really want?"
- "Why do I want this?"
- "What will it cost?"
- "Am I willing to pay the price?"
- "Am I willing to pay the price now?"

These are the questions you must be willing to answer. Of course, if you answer "no" to the that last question, the previous questions are useless.

(3) Enter the "No Whining" Zone.

"Whatever it takes" people know how to handle their feelings. They put their attitude in charge of their emotions. We all experience times when we feel bad. Our attitude cannot stop our feelings, but it can keep our feelings from stopping us. Whiners want to feel good before they do something. Winners do something so they can feel good! You can't moan and succeed at the same time.

(4) Never Be Complacent.

The final attitude characteristic of whatever-it-takes people is positive discontent. Successful people are never satisfied with what is. They see what could be, and they continually seek to achieve it. This is what drives them to get better, to achieve more, and expand into new territory. The future belongs to people who are dedicated to making their world, other people, and themselves better.

Positivity has power. W. Clement Stone said, "There is little difference in people, but the little difference makes a big difference. The little difference is attitude. The big difference is whether it is positive or negative."

4. I Choose to Be Persistent.

Everything worthwhile is uphill all the way. Network marketing presents many wonderful benefits for you, but they are all found uphill. Like any business, your success will be a result of your hard work over a long period of time.

These two words can always be found together: *persistent* and *commitment*. Never have you seen a persistent person who lacked commitment, and never have you seen a committed person who wasn't persistent. Put those two words together in your life and when you can't find a way, you'll make a way.

During a difficult time in my career I began to sense that my commitment was not enough to handle the pressures of my rocky season. I began to hesitate, question myself and pull back.

A friend gave me this quote by W. H. Murray. It encouraged me to push forward. Every day, for almost a year, I read these words aloud to myself. I pass them on to you for encouragement as you climb the hill towards your dreams:

COMMITMENT IS THE KEY
by W.H. Murray

Until I am committed there is a hesitancy, the chance to draw back. But the moment I definitely commit myself then God moves also and a whole stream of events begin to errupt.
All manner of unseen incidents, meetings, persons and material assistance that I could have never dreamed would come my way begin to flow toward me...the moment I make a commitment.

When you're committed to the uphill climb, it helps to have a path to follow. As someone who's traveled uphill for years now, I want to share with you what

I call "The Path of Persistence." People who ultimately succeed follow this path and...

Persist Through Difficult Times. For myself, I call these tough times "Seasons of Struggle." They happen to everyone. When I'm going through them, I always remind myself that "this too shall pass." Those words were birthed in my spirit during a very difficult time. My mentor, Robert Schuller said to me, "Tough times never last, but tough people do." Remember those words as you go through your "seasons of struggle." Any time you do something new you should expect to struggle. As you embark on your Network Marketing journey, if you're not struggling you're not learning. Struggle is not negative, it's positive. Struggle can and should be productive. To struggle is normal. Having a positive attitude allows it to become a positive experience.

Persist Through Failure. I wrote the book *Failing Forward* to encourage readers to persist through their failures. In the book, I candidly talked about my failures and how I got through them. When finished, I thought to myself, "Okay, Maxwell—you've written your one book on failure." Then thirteen years later I wrote *another* book on failure! What happened? With every setback in my life (and they are plentiful), I've learned more about myself and my life. Instead of seeing a failure as a tombstone, I see it as a steppingstone. When I come to a dead end in my journey, I embrace the opportunity to back up and find another way—often a better one! Success is the reward for continually learning from failure, and as you persist you rise above your "Seasons of Struggles." You'll face similar challenges in your Network marketing organization, and when it happens, don't count your losses, count your lessons!

Persist Through Criticism. Napoleon Hill wrote, "One way to avoid criticism is to do nothing and be a nobody. The world will then not bother you." But who wants to do nothing and be a nobody? Not you! Early in my career I wanted to please everyone. I quickly discovered that was not possible. My desire to grow myself and grow my business did not please a lot of average people. I wish then I would have known this wisdom from the cartoon, *Dilbert*. When faced with a coworker's displeasure, Dilbert's response was classic: "I can only please one person per day. Today is not your day. Tomorrow isn't looking good either." That might seem silly to say, but in your Network Marketing business there will be many people wanting different things from you. Others will criticize you and try to discredit your desire to advance your life. It will be up to you to realistically view where the criticism is originating from and to stay on course when distracted people become distractions for you. Remember the 5% Rule. No matter what you do, 5% of the people won't be happy. That's not a problem, that's a fact of life. This rule reminds you that criticism will always exist, so don't let it stop you from reaching your dream.

Persist Through Rejection. All of us can relate to Snoopy's response in an old Peanuts cartoon: "It doesn't make any difference whether you win or lose – until you lose." Here is what I know about rejection—none of us like it, BUT with the right attitude rejection stimulates reflection that makes us better! When you realize that most people live a life of "No," it's easier to adopt the right attitude to their persistent rejections. The right attitude takes their "No" and gives them an opportunity to say "Yes" because while most people will still say "No" that sometimes really means "Not yet." When we persist in living with the right attitude toward rejection, we quickly learn to find the people who will say "Yes" and will continue to say "Yes." One final thought on persistence: People who say "I wish" and people who say "I do" are worlds apart!

Bottom line: choose persistence. It pays.

5. I Choose to Believe in Myself and My Purpose.

Behavior follows belief. You must build a strong belief in yourself and your purpose if you wish to grow your Network Marketing business. Often, we associate belief with our dream, but allow me to go a little deeper on this thought:

Your *dream* is about *where* you want to go.
Your *purpose* is about *why* you want to achieve your *dream*.
So, when you find your *why*, you will find your *way*.

My purpose is to daily add value to people. My dream is to someday be recognized for doing that. My purpose is the reason I take the journey, and that is fulfilling. Someday perhaps I will be recognized for what I have accomplished. That is fun, but less fulfilling. My discovery? The journey really is the dream.

Too often, people confuse success with recognition. Your decision to join this Network Marketing organization has already started you on your success journey. If you do things needed to be successful daily, you are already successful! It just hasn't "showed up" yet.

Belief in yourself gets you started. Belief in your purpose gives you the reason to keep going. Too many people start a business with low belief in themselves or their purpose. The result? They seldom go beyond "the start".

Let's do a quick exercise. Using a scale of 1 to 10 (10 being highest), rank the following:

My Personal Belief Rating: ____

My Purpose Belief Rating: ____

If you want to succeed, your personal belief number should be at least a 7. Your purpose belief number should also be a 7 or higher.

All too often, a person will have a *personal* belief number that is low and a *purpose* belief number that is high. Or the opposite happens: a high personal belief and low purpose belief.

Either way, know this: for you to succeed your *personal* belief and your *purpose* belief must both be high. Here's why.

- Low Personal Belief and Low Purpose Belief = You Won't Get Started.
- High Personal Belief and Low Purpose Belief = You Won't Continue.
- Low Personal Belief and High Purpose Belief = You Won't Realize Your Dream.
- High Personal Belief and High Purpose Belief = You Will Reach Your Dream.

If your numbers are low, take some time to think about why. Then review this chapter and check out the books in the recommended reading list at the end of this chapter for ideas on how you might improve.

Your mindset choices will determine your future, so stop thinking "Can I?" and start thinking "How Can I?" When you think "Can I?" you leave room for quitting or never starting. When you ask, "How Can I?" you create room for action.

Brendon Bouchard said, "Amplifying what is great within you will accelerate your life faster than fixing what you think limits you." A positive mindset will always amplify your business and your life.

MINDSET CHOICES THAT MATTER

As you review the following mindset choices, evaluate yourself on a scale from1-5.

____ I Choose to Be Realistic.
____ I Choose to Be Coachable.
____ I Choose to Be Positive.
____ I Choose to be Persistent.
____ I Choose to Believe in Myself and My Purpose.

How did you do? The better your mindset, the higher your total number will be.

EXERCISE: A • C • T

Apply **-** What is the most important lesson I need to Apply to myself in this Chapter on the Power of Mindset?

____

____

____

____

____

Change **-** What is the most important thing I need to Change in my life from this Chapter on the Power of Mindset?

____

____

____

____

____

Teach **-** What is the most important thing I need to Teach others from this Chapter on the Power of Mindset

____

____

____

____

____

OTHER BOOKS BY JOHN C. MAXWELL YOU MAY FIND HELPFUL IN DEVELOPING YOUR MINDSET:

Leadership Gold

Success 101

Attitude 101

Failing Forward

Put Your Dream to the Test

POWER #4
LEADERSHIP

As with most careers, in Network Marketing you will never build success on your own—you will always need other people. Sometimes you will lead them, and sometimes they will lead you. But no matter what, you must make leadership a power you develop. Leading matters.

I've studied and taught leadership for over 40 years; it's the topic I'm best known for. During that time, millions of people have heard me say three core statements or read them in my books:

- "Leadership is influence – nothing more – nothing less."
- "Everything rises and falls on leadership."
- "How well you lead, determines how well you succeed."

All three describe my leadership journey, and represent my philosophy of leadership, so let me elaborate on each of these quotes.

"Leadership is influence nothing more – nothing less."

Learning how to influence others is the starting place in your leadership journey. The obvious question is, "How do you gain influence with people?" The answer is intentionally adding value to them. That's how I began.

I faced a lot of leadership liabilities. I was very young, lacked experience, had no wins under my belt and had no credibility as a leader. However, what I could do was intentionally, daily, add value to others. Soon I discovered the relationship between continually adding value to people and increasing my influence with them. They began to gather around me because I was an addition to their lives.

Leadership can be an intimidating word. Adding value to others is not. Your Network Marketing organization helps you have different ways to add value to others. Introducing people to the business will allow them to receive all the benefits that I wrote about in chapter one. Every time someone experiences one of those benefits, your influence with them will increase.

"Everything rises and falls on leadership."

Obviously, you want to add value to others and raise them up to a higher level. For that to happen, you must realize that your leadership matters. You have the opportunity of making things better for those around you. What a privilege!

"How well you lead determines how well you succeed."

That phrase describes the "Law of the Lid." Your leadership ability is the lid that determines the success of your business. For example, if your leadership ability is a 4, your business can only become a 3. Your leadership lid, for better or worse, always determines your business success. The great news is that you can lift your leadership lid! Every time you raise your lid number, your business follows.

LEADING YOURSELF

I am frequently asked, "John, what is your greatest leadership challenge?"

My answer?

"Leading myself."

Before you can lead others well, you need to know how to lead yourself well, so that's where we will begin. Winners win the personal battles of leading themselves daily. This gives them the credibility and moral authority to then lead others. It's much easier to tell people what *they* should do than to do it *myself*. My greatest challenge every day is doing what I should do, not what I want to do.

But as is often the case, my greatest challenge, gives me my greatest victories. When I lead myself well, everything else good flows out from there.

Leading myself well requires continual personal reflection and evaluation. If I'm going to "up my game" I need to make certain that I do these three things well:

1. Live Intentionally- Stop Accepting Your Life. Start Leading Your life.

The first step in leading your life is to take control of it. The opposite of that is just accepting your life as it is. Here is what that looks like:

- Hoping that everything will "work out."
- Thinking that someone or something will "make your day."
- Allowing others to have more control over your life than you.
- Waiting for others to initiate action.
- Giving responsibility for your potential best life to someone else.

That is not what you want for yourself. Perhaps that is why you have chosen Network Marketing as a career. Certainly, this industry will help you make the move from accepting your life to leading it. But you are responsible to make this shift. Here is how you do that:

Realize there is no "perfect moment" to start. People who just accept their lives are always waiting for the right time to begin. They are always getting ready to get ready. Instead of ready, aim fire, they are stuck on ready or aim and *never* fire. The job that is never started always takes the longest to get finished. Recently I was on a panel of highly successful people at a Horatio Alger event. Sitting beside me was Daniel Lubetzky, the founder of Kind™ bars. When asked a question regarding his success he said, "I'm not an optimist, I'm an actionist. While everyone else is thinking negative or positive about something, I'm taking action on it." That kind of mentality set's people up for what I call a "Pre-Win." That "Pre-Win" is taking action-getting into the game, not the results. You have to get into the game to have any chance of winning the game!

Be intentional and turn good intentions into good actions. Intentional living is the bridge between what you want to do and what you actually do. There is a difference between a life of good intentions and an intentional life. Most people want to make a significant difference; few people do. Why? Almost everyone has good intentions. Very few follow up with good actions.

My own journey began in the "almost everyone" category. My intentions were inconsistent and too many times were just thoughts—great ideas but not backed with actions. To make that turn, my intentions needed to be supported with actual activities reinforced by intentional living.

But how could I do that? I sat down and listed words that described my good intentions. Visually seeing them reaffirmed my heart but also reminded me that those words were not enough to get me to the results I searched for. Then I wrote down words of intentional living. The list looked something like this:

WORDS OF GOOD INTENTIONS	WORDS OF INTENTIONAL LIVING
Desire	Action
Wish	Purpose

Someday	Today
Fantasy	Strategy
Hopefully	Definitely
Passive	Active
Occasional	Continual
Emotion	Discipline
Somebody Ought To	I Will

When I studied both sides, it was quickly obvious that although these words in the two different columns were close on the page, there was a wide gap in the results each would bring.

But how could I cross over that span?

That's when I built the bridge of accountability. Every day I would look at the words in both columns and check whether my actions fell under good intentions or intentionality.

Study the list above and take a moment and ask yourself: "Do I live in the land of good intentions or intentional living?"

Intentional living helps you do something for yourself today that your future self will thank you for. Accepting your life will give you a future filled with regrets. Leading your life will give you a future full of results.

2. Exceed Expectations- Stop Doing Only What Is Expected. Start Doing MORE Than Expected.

As you start your Network Marketing business you have high expectations about what this opportunity will do for you. Stop right now and change your expectations from how the business will help you to how you will help the business! Why? It will allow you to get control of what you can control ... You!

You set your standards high for yourself before you set them for others. For many years I have read the following words of Dianna Snedaker, executive vice president and chief marketing officer of First Republic Bank, and tried to live up to them:

SET YOUR STANDARDS HIGH
by Dianna Snedaker

Set your standards high and keep them high. If you are interested in success, it's easy to set your standards in terms of other people's accomplishments. And then let other people measure you by those standards.
But the standards you set for yourself are always the most important. They should be higher than the standards anyone else would set for you, because in the end you have to live with yourself, and judge yourself, and feel good about yourself. And the best way to do that is to live up to your highest potential.
So set your standards high and keep them high, even if you think no one else is looking. Somebody out there will always notice, even if it's just you

You know you are leading your life when no one has to set the bar of expectations for you. Whatever others expect from you, you expect more from yourself. This is how I do it:

1. **Set the Bar** – Always place it higher than anyone else.
2. **Declare the Bar** – Let your expectations of yourself be known to others.
3. **Hit the Bar** – Back up your words with results.
4. **Raise the Bar** – Today's accomplishment won't meet tomorrow's challenges.
5. **Hit the Bar Again** – This is when people stop watching and start following.
6. **Raise the Bar Again** – The is where legends live!

My favorite story of exceeding expectations and what it looks like comes from Anson Dorrance, the legendary University of North Carolina woman's soccer coach. He was driving to work early one morning and as he passed a deserted field, he noticed one of his players off in the distance doing extra training by herself. He kept driving but he later left a note in her locker: 'The vision of a champion is someone who is bent over, drenched in sweat, at the point of exhaustion when no one else is watching.'

The young woman who received that note was Mia Hamm, who would go on to become one of the greatest players in the history of the sport.

Good followers do what is expected of them. Good leaders do more than what is expected of them.

3. Be Consistent- Stop Doing Important Things Someday. Start Doing Important Things Every Day.

People who lead themselves well prioritize well and stay consistent. Here is how it works:

- Consistency without Priorities = Not Successful but Dependable
- Priorities without Consistency = Successful Sometimes
- Priorities with Consistency = Successful Continually

Or, as I love to phrase it, "consistency compounds." Steady, daily gains produce a snowball effect after time. There are three ways consistency can benefit you in your Network Marketing business.

1. Consistency Establishes Your Reputation.

Anyone can be good once in a while. The success separator among people is consistently being good.

Cal Ripken is in the Baseball Hall of Fame. He set a record that will never be broken. He played in 2,632 consecutive baseball games. For over 16 years he came to the ballpark and played. He received the longest and loudest ovation ever given to a ball player the night they honored him for his consistency.

Which of the 2,632 games put him in the Hall of Fame? Which game caused the crowd to stand and cheer for 17 minutes? ALL OF THEM!

The Network Marketing industry rewards consistency. A fast start in this business will turn heads; however, consistency will turn profits. No one ever quit their way to the top. Doing the right things every day will give you the right results. The Power of Five only becomes powerful with consistency.

2. Consistency Is the Prerequisite to Excellence.

We are never good the first time. It takes several times before we show improvement. In fact, Malcolm Gladwell says that to achieve star status of excellence, you need to do something 10,000 times! How do you arrive at that number? Consistency.

Doing the right thing consistently maximizes your life. Average people go to the game and then leave the game. Leaders get in the game and stay in the game. Success is more about what you do than what you know.

In your industry, everyone gets training, but not everyone gets equal value from it. Everyone gets exposure, but not everyone gets equal value from it. Everyone gets relationships, but not everyone gets equal value from them. Everyone gets encouragement, but not everyone gets equal value from it. Everyone gets resources, but not everyone gets equal value from them.

So what's the difference? Exceptional leaders make the most of their opportunities, and as a result can be described as "amazing." Becoming amazing is the result of doing the right things consistently:

- Practicing is not Amazing
- Studying is not Amazing
- Trying is not Amazing
- Showing Up is not Amazing
- Asking Questions is not Amazing
- Changing is not Amazing
- Working is not Amazing
- Failing is not Amazing
- Trying Again is not Amazing

Individually these things are typical. Combined and done consistently, they become exceptional. When they are pursued with passion and a desire to ultimately add value to others, they become amazing!

Those at the top of your Network Marketing organization are models of consistency. They didn't get there quickly or easily. It has taken them years to become an "overnight" success.

You watch them lead thousands and you say to yourself, "I would like to do what they do."

You listen to them speak and you say to yourself, "I would like to do what they do."

You stand to your feet as the crowd recognizes their accomplishments and you say to yourself, "I would like to do what they do."

You see their financial success and you say to yourself, "I would like to do what they do,"

But do you ever stop to ask yourself, "Am I willing to do what they *did* so I can *do* what they do?"

They consistently did what they did thousands of times so that today they get to do what they do!

3. Consistency Compounds.

Do you know the return of doubling a penny in 31 days?

7th Day … .64 cents

14th Day … $81.92

21st Day … $10,485.76

28th Day … $1.3 million

31st Day … $10.8 million!

It takes time for the little things to add up to big things! If you wanted to melt an ice cube and the temperature was 28°, nothing would happen. Raise it to 29° and still nothing. Bump it to 30°...nothing. Even at 31°... nothing. But at 32°...something happens. The ice begins to melt. Your work without results is not *wasted* (at 28°, 29° , 30°, 31°), it's *stored.*

Consistently stored work compounds!

If you are persistent you will gain success. Momentum is the result of many pushes, not just one. Excellence is the result of many practices, not just one! If you are consistent you will keep succeeding. Martial artist and philosopher Bruce Lee was right when he stated, "Long term consistency trumps short term intensity."

You lead yourself when you live intentionally, exceed expectations, and harness consistency. And the result of doing these three things is you move away from the lesser things in life and begin leading yourself intentionally towards the greater things.

LEADING OTHERS

Once you've committed to leading yourself first, you can begin to lead others. If the thought of leading others seems intimidating, just think of it as influencing others.

Why? *Because leadership is influence, nothing more and nothing less.*

If you have any influence with anyone, you have the foundation for leading them. In this section you will learn how to increase your influence with others. As that happens, your leadership potential will increase.

In your Network Marketing organization, you will be given a position. That does not make you a leader, but it does give you an opportunity to influence others which in return will determine your leadership.

Position is optional. Influence is essential. Leadership is crucial.

If you want to use your influence with other effectively, there are four Ls you need to consider and embrace.

1. Live What You Say.

Gandhi said, "Be the change you want to see in the world." People do what people see. Setting a good example is essential for being a good leader.

In my book, *The 21 Irrefutable Laws of Leadership*, the Law of Buy-In says, "People buy into the leader before they buy into the vision." That buy-in is only possible when your words and your life match.

As a young leader, I wanted to increase my influence with others. A mentor helped me tremendously with this advice: "John, what you say must be backed up by what you do."

Out of that conversation I made an important leadership decision. If I don't believe it, I won't do it, and if I don't live it, I won't ask others to do it. Today, I still live out that important decision! My definition of a hypocrite is simple: a person who asks others to do what they won't do themselves.

Wallace Wattles said, "The world needs demonstration more than instruction." I agree. The best way to make your words and actions match is to fill your inner life with good values. When you learn and live out good values your positive influence is attractive to others.

When others see good values in you such as character, commitment, teachability, initiative, servanthood, positive attitude, personal growth and responsibility, they will be able to develop those characteristics in their lives. Stanford Research says that 89% of what we learn is visual. Living good values allows you to say to others, "Follow me," and then show them the way.

One of my first discoveries as a young leader was when I went to a new job. My words carried more weight than my actions because the people did not know me. Over time, as they began to know me better, the weight of my influence with them shifted from what I said, to what I did. That is why some people only follow leaders a short time. They are attracted to what they say but become disillusioned when the leader's actions do not live up to their words. Your Network Marketing business will flourish when your words and actions match.

2. Lift People by Adding Value to Them.

My passion to be a leader and to develop other leaders began in 1974. I became convinced that "everything rises and falls on leadership." Today my passion is much greater because I know that statement is true!

The best thing that can happen to people is good leadership. The worst thing that can happen to people is bad leadership. Leadership is influence. Positive influence blesses others while negative influence curses them.

I like to use a visual to help leaders know the effects of either pushing their people down or pulling them up. I will bring someone up on stage and have them stand beside me, then I place my hands on their shoulders and slowly push them down. To do this I have to bend down with them, and the audience can see that I reduce my stature by pushing the other person down.

But when I begin to lift that individual up, the audience sees something different. They see that as I lift the other person, I begin to rise also. Everyone can easily see that what I do to others as a leader affects both of us.

Never forget that, as a leader, you're either someone's weight or someone's wings. I choose to be wings—which is why I practice my "Daily Lifting Game Plan." Every day, I ask myself these questions to put myself in the lifting spirit:

"Who will I add value to today?"
"What do I think they need from me?"
"What can I say that will encourage them?"
"What can I do that will help improve their life?"
"What am I learning that I can share with them?"

"What am I doing that would inspire them?"
"After we are together, will they know I added value to them?"

3. Love the People You Lead.

One of my favorite Charlie Brown lines is "I love mankind. It's people I can't stand." I've known a lot of leaders like that. They love the crowd more then they love the person. That philosophy won't work for leaders, because leadership begins with one, not the masses. Every individual you lead is constantly asking three questions about you:

"Does my leader like me?"
"Can my leader help me?"
"Can I trust my leader?"

Two of those questions are relational. Relationships are the foundation of leadership. Without good relationships, leaders are tempted to manipulate people, and manipulating people is motivating others for personal advantage. The leader wins. The people lose. That is always wrong.

Good leaders motivate people for mutual advantage. The leader wins and the people win. Loving people will always cause you to motivate them not manipulate them.

Network Marketing organizations excel in this area. They are family. The atmosphere of encouragement creates a warmth that keeps alive your hopes and dreams. Their desire for your success, and for you to be your best, allows you to achieve things you would have never thought was possible.

How does that happen? By combining love with leadership.

4. Look for Potential Leaders to Mentor.

This chapter has given you the foundation to become a very good leader. We've talked about leading yourself well and we've talked about leading others well. But there's a higher leadership level we should seek when leading others:

Finding potential leaders and then mentoring them to reproduce other leaders! I call this process, "The Leader's Greatest Return." Here's a quick breakdown of how it works:

Finding Potential Leaders:

- Look for people who produce results.

- Look for people who like to help others.
- Look for people who are personally growing.
- Look for people who attract people to themselves.
- Look for people who want leadership responsibilities.

Mentoring Potential Leaders:

- Be the example of leadership. People do what people see.
- Help them to lead themselves first.
- Practice together The 4 L's of Leadership.

I love this variation on Benjamin Franklin's words: if we TELL them they will FORGET. If we SHOW them they will REMEMBER. If we INVOLVE them they will CHANGE!

One of the members of the Ambassador program, someone who has achieved quite a lot in the industry, shared a great story that sums up why leadership matters. Years ago, after the Ambassador had lost her dream home due an unexpected financial challenge, she started her Network Marketing business as a way to recover. But she was so depressed by what she'd lost that she couldn't focus on what she needed to build.

Her mentor in the business came to her one day, hugged her, and said, "If you will do what I tell you over the next couple of years, I will help you get back your house."

The bold certainty of the mentor's words resonated with her, and for the next two years, she did everything her mentor told her to do. And not only did she pull out of her depression, she was able to rebuild—and reclaim her dream house!

Leadership matters.

And always will.

Leadership Matters Evaluation

For each of the following sections, evaluate yourself on a scale from 1 to 5 for how well you're living out each item.

Lead Yourself

____ Stop Accepting Your Life. Start Leading Your Life.

____ Stop Doing Only What Is Expected. Start Doing More Than Is Expected.

____ Stop Doing Important Things Someday. Start Doing Important Things Every Day.

Lead Others

____ Live What You Say.

____ Lift People by Adding Value to Them.

____ Love the People You Lead.

____ Look for Potential Leaders to Mentor.

EXERCISE: A • C • T

Apply **-** What is the most important lesson I need to Apply to myself in this Chapter on the Power of Leadership?

____

____

____

____

____

Change **-** What is the most important thing I need to Change in my life from this Chapter on the Power of Leadership?

____

____

____

____

____

Teach **-** What is the most important thing I need to Teach others from this Chapter on the Power of Leadership?

____

____

____

____

____

OTHER BOOKS BY JOHN C. MAXWELL YOU MAY FIND HELPFUL IN DEVELOPING YOUR LEADERSHIP:

Developing the Leader Within You 2.0

The Leader's Greatest Return

The 21 Irrefutable Laws of Leadership

POWER #5
SIGNIFICANCE

While almost everyone starts out chasing success, many experience a shift towards significance along the way. Success is mainly about myself. My career. My agenda. My possessions. My desires. Significance is mainly about others. Their dreams. Their needs. Their potential.

I've known many unfulfilled successful people, but everyone I know living a life of significance is fulfilled.

Two of my very favorite things are great food and great conversation. For years, I have made it a regular practice to come to every table and start conversations by asking questions. As people engage and share their thoughts, magic begins to happen!

I have a very good list of questions for conversation starters. One of my favorite questions is "What is your best thought on how to live a fulfilled life?"

Throughout many years, I've heard dozens of responses to that question, but there's been a familiar refrain I've detected. Over and over, I hear something along the lines of, "Intentionally add value to others every day."

That is the essence of significance!

Many years ago, I received a gift from my assistant, Eileen Beavers. As I unwrapped it, I saw that it was a book, and I was immediately intrigued by the title: *The Greatest Story Ever Told.* I couldn't wait to read it, but when I opened it, I was shocked.

The pages were blank!

Inside was a note from Eileen that read, "John, your life is before you. Fill these pages with kind acts, good thoughts and matters of your heart. You write a great story with your life."

I still remember the excitement and anticipation that surged through me when I read her words. For the first time it made me think about how I was the author of my life and I could fill every page with whatever I wanted. It made me want to be significant. It inspired me to do whatever I could to make my life matter.

THE JOURNEY TO SIGNIFICANCE

The words I wrote on those pages were about my dream of making a difference. As I reflect on them today, my journey of significance contained four thoughts. I pass them on to you because I believe you will relate to how I felt when I wrote them down.

Here are the four steps on my journey of significance:

1. "I Want to Make a Difference..."
2. "Doing Something that Makes a Difference..."
3. "With People Who Want to Make a Difference..."
4. "At a Time When It Makes a Difference."

I'd like to walk you through some of my thoughts on each of these steps and share how you can make a similar journey towards significance.

1."I Want to Make a Difference..." - Make Your Life Count

I vividly remember watching Reese Witherspoon's acceptance speech after she won the Academy Award for Best Actress for her portrayal of June Carter Cash in *Walk the Line*. Witherspoon said that people often asked June how she was doing, and she would say, "I'm just trying to matter."

Reese said she understood exactly what June meant because she too was trying to make her life matter by living a good life and doing work that meant something to somebody.

That evening I felt that Reese Witherspoon spoke words right from my heart. All my life I have wanted to make my life matter to other people. Isn't that what you want? I bet right now as you read the words, "I want my life to make a difference" it resonates within you.

My father loved people and continually added value to them. He was a leader who walked slowly through the crowd, often stopping to offer encouragement to others. People naturally migrated towards his smile and friendly wave. And when he stopped, the conversation was all about them.

As a child I would hold his hand and watch the faces of people he interacted with. After a few uplifting words, they would leave with a little more hope and energy for that day. I would say to myself, "I want to be like my dad when I grow up."

Well, I grew up, and like my father, I love to intentionally add value to others every day. By doing so, I've discovered that making a positive difference in the lives of people creates a positive influence in my life. I've experienced what I call the "Significance Boomerang!" Throw it out to others and it returns to you.

Let's look at the difference between people who experience high morale versus those who have low morale:

- High Morale People Continually Make a Positive Difference.
- Low Morale People Seldom Make a Positive Difference.
- High Morale People are Passionate About Adding Value to Others.
- Low Morale People are Apathetic About Adding Value to Other.

Life is difficult, filled with challenges and seemingly more problems than answers. If you have a heart of indifference, you will never find an answer. If you have a heart to make a difference, there is always an answer and, when you find it, you'll embrace it and share it with others.

When John F. Kennedy was President of the United States he said, "Everyone has a 'change the world' speech inside of them." That's true of you and me and those around you in your Network Marketing organization. We all believe we can make a difference, but we feel the huge chasm between where we are and where we could be.

I call it, "The Significance Gap."

Personally, I've never been able to completely close the significance gap. No matter how hard I try, there is always room for improvement. Fortunately, that does not discourage me; it simply challenges me to do these two things:

Start Small. Small differences over time make a big difference. I do not have to save the world, but I can make a difference where I live.

Start Now. There is never a perfect time to start, so start now! Now is the only time you have. We over-exaggerate yesterday, overestimate tomorrow, and underestimated today. Today matters.

2. "Doing Something That Makes a Difference..." - Find Your Purpose

Harold Kushner writes: "Our souls are not hungry for fame, comfort, wealth, or power. Those rewards create almost as many problems as they solve. Our souls are hungry for meaning, for the sense that we have figured out how to live so that our lives matter, so that the world will at least be a little bit different for our having passed through it."

Those words express exactly how I felt as a young man. I was hungry to make my life matter!

The question was not "Could I make a difference?" My heart would help me do that.

The question was "What kind of difference can I make?"

To answer that question, I had to find my purpose. Here is what I discovered:

(1) Start with One Word.

When you think of making your life count, what is the one word that best describes you? This will take some time, but this exercise will give you a great return. To get to that one word, write down five that seem to best describe you. Then, thoughtfully begin eliminating words until you get to the "one word." When I did this exercise, my five words were serve, give, share, lead and work. After many discussions with people who knew me well and a lot of personal reflection, I selected the word "lead" for myself. That word became the foundation for my purpose in life. That word now had my full attention and intention. My discovery? What I focus on expands.

(2) Ask Yourself Two Questions.

The first question you have to ask yourself is, "What is my passion?"

A mentor of mine gave me this question to help me discover my passion. He asked me, "John, if you could do anything you wanted to do and be anything you wanted to be, what would you do and be?" After much time, my answer was, "I would be a leader who adds value to people." Wow! I've been doing that for almost fifty years! I challenge you to ask yourself this first question, and spend time working out your answer. Once you've done that, you can move on to the second question I asked myself, which was "What are my strengths?" You have a few abilities that make you unique. What are they? Find them. You were created for a purpose and given abilities that will enable you to accomplish that purpose. Once you discover your strengths, commit yourself to daily improve in those areas. This will make your strengths stronger and set you up for success in living out your purpose.

(3) Write Your Purpose Statement.

A purpose statement is a written down reason for being and doing. Clarity is power. Once you are clear about why you live on this earth, then whatever you do becomes a means to accomplishing your mission. My purpose statement is to "Add value to leaders who multiply value to others." Everything I do includes my purpose statement. My companies add value to leaders every day who multiply value to others. When I speak, I intentionally add value to leaders who multiply value to others. When I write books, I add value to leaders who multiply value to others. That is why I am so excited about this book. I've already shared with you my respect for the Network Marketing industry. It is out of that respect plus having discussions with many of my leader-friends in this industry, that the idea of writing this book was birthed. We asked ourselves, "What would happen if every person in Network Marketing had a book that would help them understand and do the essentials of this industry? Here it is: The Power of 5! Once again, I'm following my purpose of adding value to current and future leaders who will multiply value to others, including you!

(4) Take Action Every Day on Your Purpose.

In the movie *Pay It Forward,* Mr. Simone challenged his class to make a difference in the lives of others. He looked at his students and challenged them with these words, "Think of an idea to change our world, then put it into action." He realized that most people, in their desire to do something significant, never bridge the space between knowing and doing." Richard Bach who wrote *Jonathon Livingston Seagull*, has a single test to determine whether your mission in life is accomplished: "If you're alive, it isn't!" I assume if you are reading this, you are still alive. So ... get busy. Find your purpose and practice it every day. Someone is waiting for you to make a difference in their life.

3. "With People Who Want to Make a Difference..." - Join a Team

It didn't take long in my significance journey to discover two things: I could make a difference by myself, but I could make a bigger difference with others. What I could do was limited. What we could do was unlimited!

Mother Teresa understood the value of a team. She said, "I can do things that you cannot do. You can do things that I cannot do. Together we can do great things."

You are a part of a networking team that wants to make a positive difference in your life and the lives of others. Few people are successful unless a lot of people want them to be. With this team you are setting yourself and others up for significance. It marks a big step in your maturity and development when you realize that other people can help you do a better job than you could do alone.

It was within a team experience that I enjoyed some of my greatest wins. In that environment I was ...

- Encouraged to develop a personal growth plan
- Challenged to start writing books
- Given my definition of leadership
- Made aware of a big opportunity in the business community
- Invited to start a coaching company
- Convinced to follow my heart for country transformation

All these things happened to me because I was a part of a team that wanted to make a difference! Teams committed to significance may not be equal in experience, talent, or education but they are equal in commitment. Teams can simply do more than an individual.

In his book, *Team Building: An Exercise in Leadership,* Robert B. Maddux lists seven things that a team member needs from the coach in order to be effective:

1. A basic understanding of his or her job and its contribution to the team.
2. A continuing understanding of what is expected from him or her.
3. The opportunity to participate in planning change and to perform in keeping with team abilities.
4. The opportunity to receive assistance when needed.
5. Feedback to know how well he or she is doing.
6. Recognition and reward based on his or her performance.
7. The right work in a climate which encourages self-development.

It's true that one is too small a number to achieve greatness. A company is known for the people it keeps. Those who stay and succeed on your Network Marketing team know and live out this thought: "The best wins are when others win." Significance is all about helping others win. As I look back at my team experiences my greatest wins have been the friendships that have been formed with those who were on my team. Nothing is better than working hard together and winning big together.

4. "At a Time When It Makes a Difference." - Be Significant Now

Significance is misunderstood. People put off chasing it because they believe it requires a title, a position, money, authority, credibility, status, experience or success. But that's simply not true!

The "Steps of Significance" in this chapter are not about *any* of those things. Significance is about having a desire to add value to others that makes a positive difference in people's lives. If that's you, then it's time to get started.

My friend, all you have is *now*. In fact, there will never be another now. Don't lose today looking for tomorrow.

There are two words that will help you seize each significant opportunity: *positive anticipation*. Simply put, the moment you think your actions will have a positive outcome is the moment you take action. If you have *negative* anticipation, you will procrastinate.

Positive anticipation is empowering. It gives you permission to move through the world with expectation, which produces results. Here are some positive anticipation thoughts you should embrace as you journey towards significance in this industry:

(1) Being a Part of This Network Marketing Organization Will Be a Win/Win.

Significance is all about adding value. Your organization will add value to you and you will add value to your organization! That's essential to have a healthy business relationship. When these relationships become one-sided, they begin to fall apart. The one who gives much begins to resent the one who gives little. You will be surrounded by teammates who want to help you succeed. They will give you their best. Show gratitude by giving your best.

(2) There Will Be an Abundance of Opportunities to Do Significant Acts.

Anticipation is the key that unlocks the doors of significance. "Doors?" you may be asking. "Don't you mean door?" No, I mean doors. Abundance thinking opens many doors to abundance living. Anticipation encourages you to unlock as many doors of significance as possible. Each person that you add value to will lead you to others. Helping one is the catalyst of helping many. Do for one what you wish you could do for many and soon you will have opportunities to help many.

(3) Living the Power of 5 Daily will Empower You and Others.

The principles we've explored in this book all work together to empower you to create a life of significance. Your personal growth, mindset, and ability to lead yourself will help you make a positive impact through connecting, leading and working with others. They are the key ingredients that allow you to add value to others, and that is a recipe for a significant life. Anticipate success and meaning in your life by actively pursuing the Power of 5 every day.

You have the opportunity to live a life of incredible significance, and the good news is you don't have to wait to get started. You can make your life count by finding your purpose, joining a team, and choosing to live significance now.

EXERCISE: A • C • T

Apply **-** What is the most important lesson I need to Apply to myself in this Chapter on the Power of Significance?

____

____

____

____

____

Change **-** What is the most important thing I need to Change in my life from this Chapter on the Power of Significance?

____

____

____

____

____

Teach **-** What is the most important thing I need to Teach others from this Chapter on the Power of Significance?

____

____

____

____

____

OTHER BOOKS BY JOHN C. MAXWELL YOU MAY FIND HELPFUL IN DEVELOPING YOUR SIGNIFICANCE:

Leadershift

The 17 Essential Qualities of a Team Player

The 21 Indispensable Qualities of a Leader

Your Roadmap to Success

/ CONCLUSION /

THE POWER OF 5

This book started with my observations about the benefits of Network Marketing. If you remember, I said that Network Marketing will:

1. Make You a Better Person.
2. Add Value to Those Around You.
3. Enhance Your Income.
4. Develop Life-long Relationships.
5. Provide You Options for Your Life.
6. Start You on a Level Playing Field.
7. Expose You to Incredible Experiences.
8. Allow You to be Part of a Great Team.
9. Let You Learn While You Earn.
10. Increase Your Influence.

To maximize these benefits for your life, let's review the five essential things you must consistently do.

These five things matter.

To you.

To your business.

To others.

THE POWER OF 5

Every day I will...

GROW...because Growth Matters

CONNECT... because Connection Matters

THINK SUCCESSFULLY...because Mindset Matters

LEAD...because Leadership Matters

ADD VALUE...because Significance Matters

I've shared how I was encouraged to write my own story of significance, and it's my privilege to pass that torch to you. You already have a good start. You are considering becoming, or have become, part of an organization that will help you write an incredible story. In fact, they will be a part of it.

No matter where that story takes you, be sure to include the things that will matter every day. Be sure to live out daily the Power of 5.

I believe in you and this industry. Wherever you go, I will be cheering you on, because my name is John, and I'm your friend.